Breathe Deeply
Healing Stories For The Soul

Patricia A Burke

Illustrations by
Viki Kennedy

Audenreed Press
Brunswick, Maine
1995

BREATHE DEEPLY! HEALING STORIES FOR THE SOUL.

Copyright 1995 by Patricia A. Burke

Publisher's Cataloging-in-Publication Data

1. Burke, Patricia A.
2. Breathe Deeply! Healing Stories for the Soul
3. Psychotherapy--Therapeutic Fairy Tales--Fiction
4. Spirituality--Healing Stories for the Soul
5. Psychology--Jungian Archetype--Divine Child

Library of Congress Catalogue Number 95-788148
ISBN 1-879418-95-9

Illustrations by Viki Kennedy
Book design by Patricia A. Burke

Printed on recycled paper ♻

Audenreed Press
P.O. Box 1305
Brunswick, Maine 04011
207-833-5016

To Kim

"Thank you for teaching me how to go deeper."

ACKNOWLEDGEMENTS

I would like to honor and acknowledge the following light beings for their loving support, encouragement and challenge: Kim Rosen and the members of my Delphys I and II training pods - Jenny Chirchirillo, Sharon Delaney, Bill Forbes, Amy Fradon, Barbara France, Annie Frasser, Celeste Graves, Becca Greene VanHorn, Ann Hastings, Gerri Healey, Shannon Lee Jones, Donna Kiernan, Cathie Malach, Leslie Ritter, Lynn Safrit, Suzanne Van der Wilden, and Joyce Vinson for midwifing my birth into a new life; Kamala Hope-Campbell, Ron Canning, and the dolphins and whales for their inspiration; Jim Arbuckle, who brought me a tiny newspaper ad that synchronistically led me to Audeenreed Press; and to Nancy Desilverio who told me that I would write a book of stories long before the idea was a thought form in my consciousness.

A special thanks to Ann Hastings for her supportive challenge and unwavering faith, encouragement and love; to Kim Rosen my teacher, helper and friend, who taught me how to breathe deeply and encouraged me to follow my longing to write; and to Caitlin Williams who first helped me open a door to my "inner child."

My gratitude to Julie Zimmerman for her technical support and encouragement and for holding the cooperative vision of Audenreed Press; to Irene Howe for her invaluable editorial feedback; and to Nancy Hayward for her copy-editing talent.

I would also like to thank, with my deepest love, my mother, my grandmother, and my elementary school teachers who sparked my imagination and enchantment with fairy tales and myths by reading aloud to me when I was a child.

Finally, I would like to acknowledge and thank these eternal, blessed beings for their inspiration and teachings, Christ, the Guide, Emmanuel, Vywamus and Sepheron.

CONTENTS

PROLOGUE

The breath has been equated with "soul" or "spirit" since ancient times. Many Biblical stories, legends and myths describe God or the Goddess breathing "the breath of life" into a being's nostrils to animate, enliven, or inspire.

So perhaps you can imagine if you breathe deeply right now you might fill your lungs, not only with oxygen, but the breath of the divine presence that will saturate every cell and guide you into this moment of life. This alchemical process is what energizes the soul's journey and, in its most elemental form, is still a great mystery.

These stories explore that mystery. Through the sixth sense of the imagination and the language of metaphor, they illuminate the invisible world of the soul through the image of the "wounded/divine child," who represents the innocent part of the psyche separated from God and lost to the pain of childhood trauma and unmet needs.

This child-self, frozen in time by fear, re-emerges into the fullness of life, having grown from adversity, through an inner quest or initiation guided by a spirit helper. The child-hero returns from the journey with a commitment to living life as it unfolds, a deeper opening to relationship and a gift for the community.

In mythology that gift is known as the "hero's boon." It is the longing to belong, the desire to help others find their own way in life, and the treasure of simply being who you really are. Thus, what begins as a process of self-healing becomes a healing for the whole world.

In the honored tradition of the fairy tale, these stories seek to gently guide that frightened, child-like expression of consciousness into a greater reality where barriers and defenses are relinquished and vulnerability, the ability to touch our woundedness and follow it into the heart of bliss, becomes the breath of life that sustains the soul's journey.

Story telling is an ancient form of creative expression and teaching. Even before the written word, stories (told through pictures and dance, and in the great oral tradition of elders passing down their wisdom to youth) were the most important vehicle for transmitting history, culture, ritual, and knowledge from one generation to another. This book honors and celebrates that tradition.

One of my hopes for these stories is that they will be read aloud. I invite you to read them to your own "inner child," or to your spouse, your partner, your friends and family, or anyone with whom you long to share the gift of spoken words and expressed emotions that weave themselves into a magical offering of love and healing. I also invite you to ask someone else to read these stories to you. A gift to yourself of asking and receiving that very same offering of love.

Now, sit back, relax, and breathe deeply. Imagine the innocent part of you sitting comfortably in the lap of a trusted, loving and wise being. The voice opens, words flow and slowly, with great care, the tale unfolds and you are on your way...

WILLIAM AND THE BEAR

A ges past, in a distant land where armored knights ruled the day and there were no more dragons to slay, there lived a little-boy prince named William. William was the only son of the King and Queen of Atwa. The little-boy prince had everything his heart desired, at least that's how it seemed from the outside. Inside, he was unhappy.

After the day's jousting tournament, the King journeyed out from the fortress with his knights, into the forest and drank mead until the sun crept over the eastern horizon. When he returned home, the drunken monarch would wake his son with a hard shove and yell at him for not cleaning his room.

William's mother spent most of her time counting her jewels and scolding her intoxicated spouse. The King's response to her nagging was to ride out, once again, seeking the merrymaking in the forest, only to return the next morning with a hangover.

The Queen inevitably suffering pangs of guilt, atoned by waiting on him hand and foot, bringing cold compresses for his headache and a special tea for his nausea. Both the King and Queen then went about the day's business as though nothing had happened.

As much as his parents pretended that everything was fine, William sensed their unhappiness. *It must be something I've done,* he thought. *I must be a very bad boy.*

The little-boy prince spent much of his time alone in his room, trembling from the great weight of his shame.

One day William was rummaging around in his toy chest when he found a weathered little stuffed bear. He named the bedraggled toy Beerbear or BB for short. As William picked up the furry animal and played with him, suddenly the boy realized he felt better. He gazed at the bear, who had only one button eye, and smiled. "You make me feel happy, Beerbear, not sad or lonely or scared."

In the beginning William played with BB only when he felt bad. But then, he noticed that the more he held the bear the better he felt. So he started to bring BB with him wherever he went. Eventually, the little-boy prince wouldn't put the bear down. In fact, whenever he did, the boy felt nauseous. Then he'd quickly throw-up and pass out on his bed.

William soon realized that when he held the stuffed animal in his arms, the sick feeling would disappear. It got to the point where William needed to hold BB just to get through each day.

Soon, William was getting into fists fights with the other children when they poked fun at him and tried to steal his bear. He soon stopped playing with other children and spent as much time as he could alone in his room with his bear. BB became his best friend and his only source of comfort. The little-boy prince felt worthwhile when Beerbear was close by.

Then William started to make excuses and lie so he could stay in his room with his bear. "Mother," he'd plead, "I can't go out and play. I have to clean my room. You know how angry Father gets when my room is messy." The Queen shrugged her shoulders, scratched her head, then left the boy alone, hoping the King would talk to him when he got home from the forest.

But the King only made things worse. "It's childish to carry around a stuffed toy at your age," the hungover monarch sneered. "Grow up!"

It was when William refused to leave his room at all that his parents became worried. William, however, simply and calmly told the King and Queen, "I'm fine. There's nothing at all wrong with staying in my room, by myself, with my bear."

Deep down inside William was not fine at all. He was afraid if he gave up his bear, he'd disappear. The King and Queen were at the end of their royal rope. They threatened William with punishment, taunted and cajoled him, trying to force the boy to surrender the stuffed animal. William refused.

Finally, the King and Queen decided to get some help for their son. The Royal Nanny packed a small bag for William. Then the King dragged the boy from his room, kicking and screaming and clutching his bear. "I'm just fine," the boy cried. "Leave me alone. I don't want to go anywhere!" The Queen followed behind, shaking her head.

They traveled a long way into the dense woods, then beyond the Great River and over the glen to the foot of Amethyst Mountain. There, in a small clearing, they came upon a log cabin, made of solid oak timber and surrounded by a fragrant and colorful wildflower garden.

William was seething inside. He thought, *they've dragged me all this way for nothing. No one can make me give up my bear!*

As they approached the cabin, the mad little boy noticed several nests tucked up underneath the eaves, filled to capacity with chirping babies. He saw unconcerned bunnies quietly nibbling the tall grass and fat chipmunks stuffing their faces with tidbits of bread and sunflower seeds that had been strewn around the yard. The little-boy prince suddenly felt less angry. He thought, *at least whoever lives here likes beautiful things.*

The King knocked on a small reddish brown door, carved with the figure of a playfully leaping dolphin. A mysterious woman in a long black cloak, embroidered with magical symbols, stepped out of the dwelling, stood before the royal family and spoke in a tone that commanded authority, but was compassionate at the same time. "My name is Manue. I am the Shaman of the mountain. I understand you are seeking help."

The King and Queen had identical expressions on their faces. The King broke the silence, "How did you know that?"

The Shaman replied, "Ah... I know many things and one of the things I know is that no one comes to Amethyst Mountain unless they are seeking help."

As doubtful as the royal parents were, there was something calming about the Shaman's presence. Besides, they had no where else to turn and didn't have a clue how to handle their son.

The King told the mysterious woman about William's bear. "We don't know what else to do," explained the frustrated man. "You're our last hope."

She listened carefully, then gestured toward her cabin, "The boy will stay with me for a while. I can help him... if he is willing to be helped."

"In exchange," the Shaman continued, "you must return home and seek help for yourselves. You must learn to look inside and change the way you relate to each other and to the boy. So when William comes home, he will return to his 'real' parents and you will be able to welcome back your 'real' son."

The King protested, "It's the boy who has the problem. We're fine."

"If you cannot promise me this," she replied, "I cannot help your son."

It was clear to the King and Queen that the Shaman would not waver. Even though they were puzzled and felt vaguely uncomfortable about the changes the mysterious woman suggested, the royal parents agreed to her terms. They said goodbye to their son, relieved he was safe and that the problem of the bear was out of their hands, turned toward home and walked down the path.

The Shaman invited William to enter and sit down. She offered him a cup of gladdenberry juice. He was suspicious. *This lady in the funny cloak,* he thought, *is going to try and convince me to give up Beerbear. Ha! Just let her try. There is no one who can make me give up my bear!* Being this sure of himself, William sat down on a large pillow and drank his juice.

Manue settled herself on another pillow, laid out several crystals of varying sizes and colors and lit a large, cylindrical red candle. The mysterious Shaman closed her eyes and telepathically conferred with the devas and nature spirits who roamed freely in her garden. Then she consulted with her special inner guide, a very wise and playful dolphin named Genie.

After she finished her ritual to create a sacred space, Manue gazed into the boy's eyes and said, "I open my heart to you, young friend, and give you my best. Please, if you will, tell me about your bear and why he is so special to you."

William was speechless. He was certain the Shaman would badger and blame him, judge and cajole him, just like everyone else. Instead, she asked him a question no one else cared to ask. Suddenly, the wall the boy had erected around his vulnerable heart began to crumble. William realized that for the first time, in a very long time, he felt safe.

The boy poured out his heart to the mysterious woman. "I'm afraid to give up my bear. He's the only thing that makes me happy. When Beerbear is in my arms, I feel worthwhile."

She listened very carefully and kept her heart open to the young child's pain. When he finished, Manue asked the boy one simple question, "If there was another way to feel good about yourself and to find some happiness in life, would you be willing to try *that* way?"

William noticed a lump in his throat. He stumbled on his words, "Well... uh... um... I, uh... I guess so." Then his voiced steadied as determination took hold, "Yes, yes, I'm willing to try another way."

Manue spoke to the boy in a soft, gentle tone, "You see, William, the bear makes you feel good for only a short while. In order to keep the good feeling you have to cling to him. The problem is, you lose everything else that's important to you, including your self. To find true happiness you must look inside, instead of outside... but you need not follow this path alone."

The Shaman stood up and walked toward an enormous cupboard, then opened the doors. Inside were rows and rows of raggle taggle stuffed bears of all shapes, colors and sizes.

She pointed to the bears, "You see, William, there are many other little boys and girls just like you. If you like, I'll introduce you to them. They'll teach you how to find happiness inside of yourself, instead of depending on Beerbear."

William hesitated, momentarily paralysed with doubt. He looked imploringly at the Shaman. Manue slipped her arm around the boy and gently squeezed his shoulder. William sighed deeply, then placed his bear on the shelf with the other stuffed toys. Salty tears streamed down his young face. "I'm really sad," he sobbed.

"I understand, William." The Shaman held the boy close. "But tell me something, is this sadness any different than the sadness you felt alone in your room?"

William thought for a moment, then said, "Yes, but I don't know why."

The Shaman explained, "What you're feeling now, my young friend, is the kind of sadness that comes when we lose something we love. If you let yourself feel it, it will be there for a while, then pass. The sadness you felt in your room, all alone, was the kind of sadness that never goes away because you kept trying not to feel it."

The boy's eyes widened. "You're right. It's different. It's not as bad as I thought it would be. It's kind of soft and mushy, not hard and jagged like those other times."

The Shaman smiled and led the boy outside to a group of laughing children who were sharing stories, chasing butterflies and playing hide and seek. They eagerly welcomed William into their circle. For the first time in his life the young boy felt happy from the inside out. He had come home to his heart.

William stayed with the Shaman at the foot of Amethyst Mountain for as long as he wanted. When he was ready to leave, he thanked all the children, the devas, nature spirits, and animal guides. Then he packed his bag with the few things he had brought with him, minus his furry bear, who was still sitting quietly in the cupboard with the other stuffed animals.

Manue walked with him through the glen, beyond the Great River, and back through the forest until they saw the castle just over the ridge. The Shaman took the boy's hands, one last time, looked lovingly into his eyes and said, "William, my young friend, it will be painful sometimes. There will be moments when you wish you still had Beerbear in your arms. When you find yourself at those points of choice, you must remember everything you've learned from the children about finding happiness from within. Then you won't need to seek comfort or fulfillment from outside. I bless you on your journey. You are always welcome at the mountain."

William gave the Shaman a hug and said goodbye. His body flowed with a new sense of freedom as he turned, headed down the path toward home, and finally slipped out of view.

THE GREAT WISE DOLPHIN

L ong ago in the ancient time of KA, before the coming of the human kin, lived a great dolphin pod in the vast ocean of Atlantia. The dolphin were a peaceful and loving species. They lived harmoniously within an ocean community of thousands of animal and plant friends and kindred spirits too numerous to mention.

As was their nature, the dolphin spent most of their time swimming straight and true along the swift currents of the open sea, the vast blue-green waters of their home. Powerful and graceful, these sleek, grey and white beings of the deep were often seen dancing in the waves with each other. If mindful, one might see a bottle-nosed beast riding another's wake, plummeting head first into a bed of kelp to avoid detection, then surprising the rest of the pod by pushing her body completely out of the water and flipping head over tail in total bliss.

Amongst this great pod lived a delightful young dolphin named Jewel. She was born of Ta and Venya. But in keeping with the custom of all dolphin pods, Jewel soon became one with the larger community. The adults shared equally in the responsibility of raising Jewel, teaching her the value of harmony, communication, and cooperation, while respecting her individual needs. She quickly learned to dance in the waves with all the creatures of the sea.

For Jewel, the most exciting time during the cycle of days was story hour. During these precious moments, the elder record-keeper of the pod gathered the young ones together to share his vast wisdom and knowledge of the universe, passed down to him through the sacred art of story-telling.

Jewel's favorite story was the myth of the Great Wise Dolphin. She'd keep her eyes glued to the record-keeper, taking note of subtle shifts in his facial expressions and listening for every nuance in his voice, ingesting each word with serious enthusiasm as if it were a tender morsel of food. The excitement built to a climax as the finale of the story approached and the record-keeper, with a flare, ended with this proclamation, "Now remember, children, the Great Wise Dolphin created all that is, and all that is created is forever joined to Her by the glow of each being's inner light."

Jewel loved this enchanting tale so much, that after each re-telling of it, she'd swim a short distance from the pod, find a calm spot on the ocean's surface, and bask in the beauty of its meaning. The young dolphin floated quietly in the profound silence of her watery world, breathing deeply, and diving inward to the core of her being. There, without exception, she'd bathe in the bliss of her own inner light and open her heart to the Great Wise Dolphin.

And so it was for Jewel. Day after day, life was one unbounded moment of joy and peace. Until... one dreadful night.

During a rest period, in the middle of a moonless night, the young dolphin floated a short distance from her pod. She found herself near a small island covered thickly with mangrove trees, their spindly, exposed roots masking the entrance to an underwater cave.

Without warning, from the depth of this hidden grotto, slithered the Jinjara. He was a wraith-like creature, with fiery, red eyes and a whispered body, elusive as a puff of smoke. Before Jewel could swim free or call for help, the Jinjara engulfed her.

The young dolphin's sleek, grey skin crawled at the menacing touch of the stranger. Overcome with fright and choked from his suffocating demeanor, panicked thoughts raced through the young one's mind. *Maybe if I lie very still and stop breathing, he'll think I'm dead and go away!*

As if the Jinjara could read her thoughts he growled at her, "I'll never go away. I am alone in my cave and I need a young, impressionable thing like you to do my bidding. You are nothing to me. Be forewarned, if you ever tell anyone what has happened here, I will punish you and destroy your puny friends. Ha! As if anyone would believe you anyway." With that, the Jinjara slithered back into his hole.

Jewel snuck silently back to her pod. Wild, untameable fear vibrated through every cell in her body. Her normally fluid motion through the waves was now halting, tentative. She longed to tell the elders of the pod about her encounter, but she believed the Jinjara's menacing warning. As Jewel faded into a semi-conscious state, floating helplessly in the vastness of Atlantia, she repeated over and over to herself, "I must not tell. I must not tell."

Night after night the Jinjara descended upon the defenseless dolphin. A powerful master of the art of shape shifting, the wraith often appeared to her in the guise of a familiar dolphin. With this ploy, the menacing stranger easily lured Jewel into his grotto, light years away from the safety of her pod. In the sheer terror darkness of his own domain, he'd have his way with her. Jewel soon doubted her own reality and fell into despair.

The young dolphin realized she could not escape the wiles of the Jinjara, nor could she ask for help. With no exit from her torment, Jewel was left with only one recourse. From that moment, whenever the Jinjara touched Jewel, the young dolphin closed the breathing spout on top of her head and swam right out of her body.

Jewel understood that this utterly unnatural act was dangerous for a dolphin, but felt she had nothing to lose. An uncontrollable shiver ran up her spine. *I must escape,* she thought. *I'd rather die than feel his awful touch!*

Free from her own body, a body she now despised, the young dolphin traveled to distant, exotic worlds, where there were no mysterious grottos, menacing strangers, nor "awful, crawly feelings." During these journeys, the young dolphin forced herself to forget the terrifying encounters with the Jinjara. Then, just as the dolphin's abandoned body had consumed its last molecule of oxygen, Jewel would come crashing back into her shell, dazed and exhausted.

As the days and nights wore on, the others noticed that Jewel was not acting at all like a dolphin. She often stayed apart from the pod, circling aimlessly, as if in a dream... looking for something she'd lost.

The young dolphin turned off her sonar, refusing to communicate. She barely ate and never danced in the waves.

The elder record-keeper approached the young dolphin, "My precious Jewel, we are all concerned about your unusual behavior of late. Is there something wrong? Can we help?" Jewel heard the tenderness in the old dolphin's voice, then noticed a deep ache push its way up from the pit of her stomach into her throat. But before she could open her mouth, the voice of the Jinjara echoed in her mind, "I will punish you and destroy your puny friends..." Jewel choked back a tear, then darted out of sight.

The young dolphin found an isolated corner of the ocean. From somewhere deep within her exhausted frame, a plaintive cry emerged, "If the record-keeper could just know what happened without me telling, the Jinjara wouldn't hurt anyone." Unfortunately for Jewel, this was wishful thinking of the sort that just doesn't come true. So she floated despondently on the cold surface of her watery world, eyes vacant, trapped in her own cage of fear.

As Jewel grew older, the Jinjara lost interest in her and ceased his rude intrusions into the dolphin's life. Although Jewel was able to bury the memory of her sickening encounters with the stranger, she remained trapped in her self-imposed isolation, ever fearful of the tiniest creature in the sea, an errant wave or sudden burst of wind.

The dolphin clutched her feelings tightly to her chest. She thought she might explode. The uninvited terror that had once visited her from the mysterious grotto now lived inside her wounded heart. In the midst of this day-to-day desolation, Jewel wondered if the last spark of her inner light had smoldered and died.

One particularly bleak day, as Jewel swam out of her body, she paused a moment to float quietly under the crystal blue sky. It was then she noticed an iridescent shape, with translucent wings, zooming towards her.

The unusual form shifted and changed as shafts of sunlight penetrated it. Jewel thought, *this isn't like any bird I've ever seen.* The young dolphin was scared, but curious, intuitively sensing this creature meant her no harm.

Suddenly Jewel noticed a vaguely familiar warmth in her heart. The dolphin's attention was drawn inward to a faint glimmer of light, burning ever so slightly brighter with each passing moment.

The multi-colored being approached Jewel and introduced herself. "Hello, my young friend. My name is Patwe."

The disembodied dolphin stared at this airy wonder. Patwe responded to the dolphin's unspoken query, "I am your spirit guide. I am an angel and have come here to remind you that you are safe. The Great Wise Dolphin has sent me to guide you back to her."

Jewel's body vibrated with excitement. Then fear crept into her heart again. "I don't know if I believe in angels. Prove it! Tell me how you found me."

Patwe was undaunted by the young dolphin's doubt. "The Great One sensed your despair and sent me to guide you home. I followed your inner light."

Jewel was stunned. "I thought it burned out long ago. My inner light still glows?"

"Yes, Jewel. It's faint, but still glows. Nothing can ever completely extinguish that flame."

Jewel pondered this turn of events. *This angel must be very clever to find me with such a faint light and my sonar turned off, too.* Jewel was impressed. She decided to listen to Patwe.

As they talked, Jewel slowly began to trust the clever angel. "Patwe, can you really help me remember my real dolphin-self again?"

"Yes, I can. I'll guide you to the Great Wise Dolphin. She has all the wisdom and love you need. But first you must return to your body. You are dangerously close to losing yourself completely up here in the ethers. Your body will waste away to nothing if you don't return soon. The only way to rejoin The Great One is through the doorway of an open heart. You must allow yourself to fully experience the feelings you have avoided for so long, to reawaken your life force. Only then will you be free to dance in the waves once more."

"Are you sure this is the only way to find my real self again?" Jewel pleaded, "Are you sure there isn't some easier way? I don't think I can do it."

Patwe gently stroked the young dolphin's heart with her angel wing and replied, "The only way through the pain is to enter into it fully. But you don't have to swim this journey alone. I'll be with you the whole time."

Finally, Jewel agreed. The angel guided the dolphin to her pod and assisted her back into her body. Jewel touched down with such a jolt that the wind was knocked from her chest.

Patwe patiently instructed the young dolphin, "Jewel, quiet your mind, breathe deeply and follow your breath through the opening in your heart. Once you cross over the threshold, your breath will guide you to your inner light. Whatever happens, keep breathing deeply and move towards the light."

Jewel closed her eyes. She sensed a faint light flickering somewhere inside. As she dove deeper and deeper into her inner experience, the light shone brighter and brighter. Suddenly, the dolphin found herself in a large expanse of water she had never seen before, but was somehow familiar.

An immense sphere of brilliant white light appeared just above the horizon. As Jewel swam closer, she noticed a dolphin figure surrounded by an aura of soft pink light. As this radiant being emerged from the center of the orb, Jewel exclaimed, "You're the most beautiful dolphin I've ever seen!"

The mystical being spoke, "I am the Great Wise Dolphin. I have been searching for your light for a very long time. I am blessed in this moment and filled to overflowing with joy that you have finally returned to me."

Jewel stumbled on her words, " Wa...wait a minute, I thought you left me!"

The Great Being smiled tenderly. "I have always been here, inside you. The moment you turned away from your inner light, you also turned away from me. My dear one, I sent Patwe to you when the moment was ripe to guide you home, to yourself... and thus, to me."

Suddenly Jewel was swept up in a flood of joyful tears. "I found you. I found me!"

A startling insight burst into Jewel's awareness. "It was me, wasn't it? I trapped myself in my own cave of fear. I tried to shut off my light and lost my connection to you."

Jewel sobbed deep sobs of sadness, joy and relief. "I'm ready to come home to myself now... I'm ready to come home to you."

The Great Wise Dolphin touched Jewel's heart with her fin and breathed new life into her. The dolphin's lungs filled to capacity, vigorously pumping, in and out, until Jewel's natural breathing pattern re-established its own rhythm.

Jewel thrashed about in the water, furiously pounding the waves with her tail. In the next moment she screamed a scream as deep as the deepest rift in the bottom of the sea, then winced as the muscles in her sleek, grey body contracted and released. This long held suffering dispersed into millions of bubbles, awakening a profound sense of vitality in her cells.

Jewel laughed a deep belly laugh, then vocalized an ecstatic pattern of rhythmic dolphin clicks. "My sonar! My voice! I have my voice again."

Jewel had flowed through each of these once terrifying feelings in a few short seconds. The joyful dolphin had, indeed, crossed over the threshold of forgetting, into a re-awakened body, where she could, now, dance to the beautiful music of her own rhythms.

Jewel shot straight up out of the water, flipped head over tail and howled, "I'm me again!"

Then Jewel noticed that her light not only burned much brighter but its warmth radiated far beyond the normal bounds of her own body. Confused, she turned once again to her wise friend, "Why does my light shine so far?"

The Great Wise Dolphin took Jewel under her pectoral fin and gently reassured her, "My precious Jewel, you are remembering your connection with all of my glorious creation. You can continue to experience this joyful union as long as you remain in your body and tuned into your own truth."

"Yes, I remember!" cried Jewel, "the Great Wise Dolphin created all that is... and all that is created is joined to Her by the glow of each being's inner light. That's the end of the record-keeper's story. It's really true!"

"Yes, my dear. It's really true!"

Soon it was time for Jewel to return to the ordinary reality of her life with the pod in the vast ocean of Atlantia. As she prepared herself for departure, The Great Wise Dolphin offered some final wisdom. "Jewel, you must tell the other dolphins about the Jinjara. This will be painful at times. Some of the pod will not believe you. Others will, for they, too, have been injured by the Jinjara. Seek out these kindred souls and gather together to share your experiences and the journey of remembering. It is there you will all find hope and new life.

If the Jinjara ever returns to you in your dreams or visions, call upon the help of Patwe or myself. Say 'NO!' to him from the depths of every cell in your body. Remember, when you say 'NO!' to the Jinjara, you are really saying 'YES!' to yourself... 'YES!' to life... 'YES' to truthful relationship with all that is."

Then the Great Wise Dolphin gazed deeply into the young dolphin's eyes. "Remember, my precious Jewel, I am always here... waiting for you, in love, with my arms wide open. Simply focus your awareness inward, breathe deeply, and follow your inner light."

With a tear in her eye and gratitude in her heart, Jewel said goodbye to the Great Wise Dolphin and returned to her ordinary life in the pod. As Jewel opened her eyes, she caught a fleeting glimpse of her angel guide. Patwe smiled, imparted a sweeping angel wave and with a flourish, flew off on gossamer wings into the sunset.

Jewel bubbled and beamed. She knew there was more healing to be done. For the moment, however, filled with a freshly awakened sense of freedom, she was content to swim straight and true along the swift currents of the open sea, basking in the warm glow of her own inner light.

BARBUDOM

M any millions of years ago, as the immense cosmic forces of the universe swirled into alignment, the blue-green sphere known to all as the Glorious Mother was born. Her aura emerged from massive, swirling clouds, teeming with tiny particles that danced with the new light. Her vast oceans churned and bubbled with the beginnings of life. From within the depths of this liquid wonderment volcanos exploded with her fiery passion, creating solid ground, where, she adorned herself with luscious jungles and teeming swamps. During this time of great beginnings, out of the primordial ooze, was born a strange and magnificent beast named BARBUDOM.

BARBUDOM was an exceedingly large creature, covered with fur and scales and feathers. He had a dragon's tail, the body of a rhinoceros, and the head of a tiger. Long, sharp talons grew from his paws and fangs the size of sabers from his jaws.

As he emerged from the Glorious Mother's womb BARBUDOM examined the unfamiliar surroundings. "Where am I?" he pondered aloud. "Why have I come to this strange place?"

The beast then looked at his own body. Suddenly, BARBUDOM's face turned a pale shade of green, his lips a deep blue. "What's this ugly shell around me?" His eyes glazed over. "I'm trapped. Get me out of here! I want to go home!"

The beast's blood began to boil, and curls of smoke seeped from his ears. In the next instant, a fearful dread crept into his belly and turned his lunch upside down. "Who am I?" he moaned. "I can't remember who I am."

BARBUDOM let out a ferocious howl. The anguished rage in his voice echoed for miles. When the reverberation returned to him, the baffled beast cried out, "What savage creature be you, who'd tear me apart and cast my bones to the wind?" There was no reply.

The silence was deafening. The fearful dread deepened in the beast's belly. BARBUDOM whimpered, then lumbered as fast as his large body would take him into the deepest part of the jungle, desperately fleeing the savage voice.

BARBUDOM stumbled upon a cave in the heart of the jungle, just big enough for him to squeeze into. The beast curled up into a tight little ball, then covered his eyes with his cumbersome paws. He lay in the darkness, shivering, the rise and fall of his chest imperceptible to the eye.

The day turned to night and the night back to day, the days into weeks, the weeks into months and the months into years. BARBUDOM did not move from that spot and never made a sound. A single thought burrowed deep into his brain, looping round and round in an endless spiral. *The Great Creator has forsaken me. He's banished me to this awful place and forced me into this detestable body as punishment. I must be the most repulsive brute that ever lived.*

As the years went by, other creatures, great and small, slowly emerged from the life-giving ooze, and one-by-one moved out and about. Some traveled deep into the jungle, others followed the path into the mountains, and still others scampered to the desert, each with the single-minded purpose of finding their own niche and adding to the beauty of the evolving sphere.

One day BARBUDOM awoke from a profound sleep. He noticed hunger gnawing at his belly and a deep ache in his heart. Suddenly his longing propelled him upward. "Ouch!" he yelled. "Now I have a nasty bump on my head. That'll teach me not to be so hasty."

In the next moment, the beast decided to venture out into the world. That familiar sense of dread crept into his cells. BARBUDOM froze. *Should I stay or should I go?* was the question rumbling around in his brain. His longing was greater than his fear. The beast placed his right front paw slightly forward. His momentum carried him out of the cave.

As BARBUDOM tentatively poked his head out into the light of day, he saw, grazing quietly next to the entrance of the cave, creatures of such beauty and grace that his heart leapt with joy. Without thinking, the beast rushed forward with wild abandon, desperately clutching at anything that moved, in the vain hope of capturing the love he craved.

Frightened by this desperate, destructive energy, the smaller animals fled. Then some of the larger animals turned on BARBUDOM. "You vile, loathsome beast," they howled, gnashing their teeth and slashing at him with their claws. "Get away from our children. Leave us alone!"

BARBUDOM was horrified and fled into the jungle. When he found a dark, safe spot he lay down and once again curled into a tight little ball. He thought a long time about why the creatures had run from him, then attacked him. One and only one conclusion was possible for the beast's under-developed brain. *I'm ugly. Everyone hates me because I'm ugly.*

BARBUDOM suddenly felt utterly alone. Then a powerful rage swelled up from the beast's belly, flooding his awareness like a tidal wave crashing the shoreline. BARBUDOM pounded the ground with his paws. He gouged large holes from the earth with his claws, then thrashed about with his dragon tail, tearing up trees from their roots. The beast stomped around in a circle, raised his fist to the sky and yelled in the general direction of where he imagined the Great Creator lived, "This just isn't fair! I'll show you... I'll make myself beautiful!"

Thinking he'd found the key to life, BARBUDOM carefully crafted an elaborate costume from vibrant green leaves and fragrant flowers of varied hues. The beast adorned himself with all the colors of the spectrum: red, orange, yellow, green, sky blue, indigo, and white. As he worked, BARBUDOM's mood changed. *This is much better,* he thought. *Now I'm the most beautiful creature on the planet. The others will fall at my feet and gaze at me in loving adoration. I'll never feel angry or lonely or frightened ever again.*

BARBUDOM decided to try out his new costume. He lumbered back to the clearing in front of his cave, his heart pounding in anticipation of meeting some new friends. As he approached, he saw several small, furry creatures scurrying about gathering nuts and seeds. The beast paused, not wanting to startle them again.

When the others saw BARBUDOM, they curiously approached this wondrous new being, not recognizing the enormous beast behind his mask. "Look," they tittered, "he's so beautiful... and smells good, too." Then one of the creatures looked more closely, sensing that something was not quite right. "Run!" he cried, "It's that terrible beast from the cave." Now frightened, they once again fled into the jungle.

BARBUDOM felt as if the world had fallen out from under his feet. "I don't understand," he cried. "I was sure this time it would be different." The beast's eyes filled with fiery tears. "I'll always be alone." A searing pain ripped through the beast's chest, then a volcano erupted in his belly.

The rage-filled beast stomped around in a circle, destroying nests, hurling rocks and ripping trees up from their roots. BARBUDOM let out a ferocious howl the likes of which no one had ever heard. The echo sounded for thousands of miles, then once again returned home. BARBUDOM shouted, "Where be you, oh savage brute? Show your face, at last. I'll face you now, even though it means the death of me!" There was no reply.

In the midst of the silence, the dread returned. He lumbered into his cave and curled up into an exceptionally tight ball. Then BARBUDOM raised his eyes imploringly to the heavens. This time instead of shaking his fist, the despairing beast prayed, "Almighty, I don't know why you've sent me here to live out my life all alone, but I need your help now. Please, I don't know what to do."

Suddenly BARBUDOM heaved a deep sob, his chest expanding beyond its fullness. A shaft of brilliant white light descended through the roof of the cave, into the top of the beast's head, into his heart, then still deeper into his very core.

Suddenly, BARBUDOM heard a powerful, yet compassionate voice, whose tone was unlike his own ferocious howl, yet very familiar to him. "I am the Great Creator within you," it said.

The beast's back stiffened. But the voice was so soothing, BARBUDOM quickly relaxed and slipped into a space of inner stillness. With great certainty the beast replied, "You are the Almighty."

Then, BARBUDOM invaded the tranquility with hundreds of questions fired in rapid succession at the Creator, "Why am I here? Why is there another beast after me? Why are the other creatures afraid of me? And most of all, I want to know how I can stop being afraid and make friends with the other animals?"

The Great Creator spoke slowly and gently to the giant beast, "My dearest BARBUDOM, you have come here to remember who you really are and bring your unique gifts to this evolving world."

"But Creator," the beast protested, "I have no gifts to offer. I'm ugly and the other creatures are repulsed by me. Some of them even attack me. Then, there's that really scary monster who lets loose such a blood-curdling howl, but never shows his face."

The Great Creator smiled, "My dearest beast, that was your own voice. You simply didn't recognize it. There is nothing to fear except that which is within you that you have not been willing to accept. When you allow yourself to experience yourself and your feelings fully, that energy will become your greatest power and gift to the world."

"Even anger?"

"Especially your anger. Deny your ferocity and others will run from you. Be who you are with loving intent and you'll find the companionship you seek."

As the Great Creator spoke, years of secret anger, swallowed up by fear, suddenly dissolved into the beast's breath. But there was one last resentment that needed to be voiced, "Why," BARBUDOM pleaded. "Why did you send me to this place, then leave me to fend for myself?" The Great Creator smiled warmly at BARBUDOM and replied, "I never left you. I've been inside you all the time. You simply forgot your true nature. You are a being of light and love, created from my essence. When you called, in love, I came."

BARBUDOM paused. He tilted his head quizzically, then a broad toothy grin crept onto his face. "Yes, yes!" The beast cried ecstatically. "I remember, now."

Then BARBUDOM let out a ferocious howl. This time, however, instead of running away, he turned toward the sound and claimed it as his own. "That's my voice," he shouted. "I can feel it in my belly. It's not so scary after all."

BARBUDOM leapt to his feet. "Ouch! Not again." The beast rubbed the throbbing lump on his head, but was too excited to notice the pain. He raced out of the cave with a new lightness and grace to his gait.

BARBUDOM stood tall in the sunlight. The other animals were no longer afraid of him. They eagerly welcomed the beast into their midst. BARBUDOM enthusiastically threw his body into a wild, yet graceful dance, then howled to his heart's content.

BARBUDOM noticed an urge rumbling around in his belly to see his own reflection. He followed his impulse to a pool of crystalline, blue water, then peered over its edge. The enormous beast was startled by his transformation. He was no longer a strange mishmash of different creatures but a handsome, powerful lion with a long golden, flowing mane.

BARBUDOM laughed a laugh the likes of which no one had ever heard. It echoed throughout the jungle, over the mountains, through the desert and down to the vast oceans of this blue-green sphere known to all as the Glorious Mother.

All the creatures gathered round BARBUDOM. They took hands and paws and claws and began to dance in a circle. Much to his delight, BARBUDOM no longer felt lonely. "At last," he sighed, "I belong."

In that moment the lion's heart burst open with love. Then all the other creatures, great and small, pronounced him king of the jungle by virtue of his great wisdom, courage, and love.

BARBUDOM opened his heart to the sky, then turned his attention inward and thanked the Great Creator, "I know, now, why I'm here."

The Almighty smiled at his dearest beast, gently reminding him, "I am always here for you. Simply call upon the power of your inner beauty and I will come."

Then the handsome beast turned to his new family and proclaimed, "Let this be a day of joyous celebration for this new creation, our Glorious Mother, our home."

All the creatures clapped, then danced and danced and danced. Then the day turned to night and the night back to day, the days into weeks, the weeks into months and the months into years. BARBUDOM and his friends never stopped dancing.

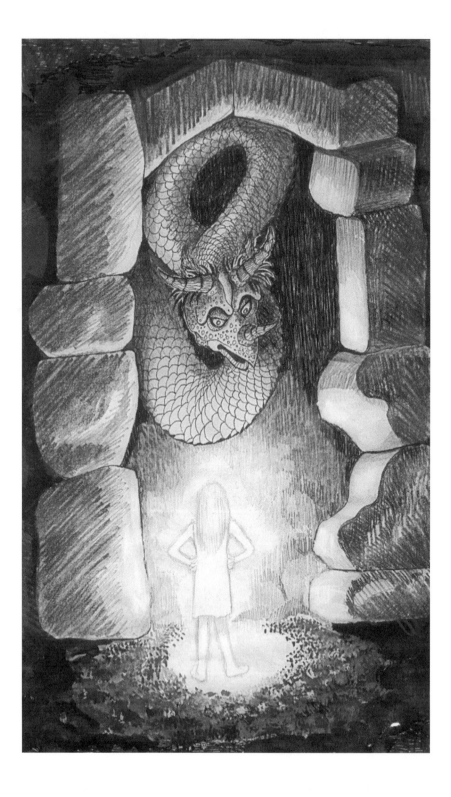

A WORLD WITHOUT DARKNESS

Long ago, in a somber age of empty pain, when joy was just a shadow in the murky consciousness of everyday folk, lived a young girl named Ariel. Ariel lived with her parents in a small clapboard cottage at the edge of a village settled deep in the gloomy depression know as the Valley of Doom. The tiny town was over-shadowed on all sides by stark, jagged mountains. The tallest of these peaks was Dragon Mountain, named after the ferocious fire-breathing monster who dwelled in the cave at the top and ruled with a fist of terror in the valley below.

The Valley of Doom was continuously covered by a thick fog, infused with a fear so intense, that when you inhaled, a shiver would run up your spine. During the day the world was grey. At night it was so dark you couldn't see a horse standing a fraction of a foot in front of your face.

Hardly anyone ever ventured out of their homes. The Dragon King frequently swooped down out of his mountain lair. He terrorized the villagers with piercing howls and snorts of fire, leaving the town scorched and smelling acrid with smoke.

Ariel was an unhappy child. She longed to go outside, play with other children and chase butterflies in the meadow behind the cottage. She couldn't accept fear.

The little girl hated that everyone talked in whispers and skulked about as if they had done something bad.

I get so mad, she thought, *that people are so afraid.* She was particularly offended when her parents yelled at her for singing. She so loved to sing light, airy, melodies. In fact, the child had the voice of an angel and could have made first soprano in any celestial choir.

Unfortunately, Ariel's parents banned her singing. "Ariel, be quiet," they'd shout in whispered tones. "If you don't stop singing, the Dragon King will swoop down from his cave and burn our cottage to a crisp!" Of course this never happened... but the fear... oh, that throat-clutching, gut-wrenching tremble of terror remained constant and unwavering.

Ariel didn't understand her parents, but she didn't want to make them more frightened and unhappy than they already were. So she stopped singing... even though it broke her heart.

Unfortunately for the child, when she silenced her voice and hid her anger, that throat-clutching, gut-wrenching tremble of terror snuck into her body like a weasel into a chicken coop. Day after day Ariel sat in a corner of her tiny cubby hole of a room, silently inhaling the fog.

One day, the girl heard a strange ringing in her ears. It sounded vaguely like music. Ariel thought she was going crazy. She lay down on her bed and breathed deep full breaths. She knew from experience that breathing eased her anxiety. In the next moment, the young girl floated gently out of ordinary reality into a dream-like state.

Ariel was startled to find herself circling above the Earth in a small capsule. *Oh my gosh,* she thought. *I'm in outer space. But I haven't left my room. How can this be?*

The girl suddenly materialized in a foreign land, in a bright city plaza, where people of all different shapes, sizes and colors were laughing and talking, without the slightest care. Best of all, there were no dragons. The young girl was delighted, and for the first time in a very long time, felt no fear.

When Ariel returned from her journey, it occurred to her that she might be able to repeat her experience if she just lay down and breathed. So every day the young girl would sneak off to her room and breathe herself into that dreamy space. These adventures gave Ariel brief moments of respite from her everyday experience.

Ariel soon realized she was traveling inside her mind. *I'm not in outer space, but inner space!* she thought, as she'd orbit the Earth in her tiny capsule, wondering what exotic land to visit next.

Often the young voyager would put on her space suit, tie herself to a life line from her ship and simply float for hours in the weightless void. From this vantage she could see billions of stars, like pin pricks of light through a dark, protective dome. Ariel loved this state of relaxation.

One day Ariel was drifting aimlessly near her space ship. She was alarmed by an odd-looking fellow who suddenly appeared from an inner-stellar nebula. As the figure floated by, Ariel burst out laughing. The being wore a flashy yellow neon wet suit and high-tech scuba gear, air tank, mask and snorkel.

Ariel began to hear the peculiar ringing noises again. The tones seemed to come from her helmet, then from right inside her head. *I must really be going crazy this time,* she thought. But then the girl noticed that the ringing was really more like music. With her curiosity now aroused, Ariel listened more closely. Suddenly she realized that the strange-looking being was singing to her telepathically through his snorkel!

Ariel was astonished. "I understand what you're saying. Keep singing, please keep singing!"

"Hello friend, I am Gleeban, from the planet Unity. I mean you no harm. I was diving into the space void to practice my breathing and here I am, surprised, however delighted, to meet another scuba enthusiast. I've never before met another diver in this part of the galaxy. Please, if you will, tell me your name and on what planet you reside."

Needless to say, the young explorer was shocked to be communicating telepathically with an extraterrestrial scuba diver in inner space... her inner space! However, Gleeban seemed to be friendly and the music was so beautiful that Ariel's anxiety soon dissolved.

Ariel wasn't quite sure how to talk to the ET. Then an amusing idea popped into her brain. *Well, I guess I'll just sing a song in my mind and see if he understands.*

Through the music in her thoughts, Ariel told Gleeban her story. She sang a lyric ballad describing in vivid detail the oppressive Valley of Doom, the Dragon King, his reign of terror and her adventures in space.

Gleeban not only understood the girl perfectly but was moved by her tale. "Please come with me, my friend," the ET sang a sweet nursery rhyme, "Come with me to Unity. We'll banish your miserable fright and ease your terrible plight."

Gleeban took Ariel's hand and sang to her telepathically as they disappeared into the nebula and reappeared at the bottom of a pool of imperial purple water. They emerged from the lake, then walked to the center of a beautiful blue meadow, where rainbow butterflies as big as bald eagles fluttered through the clear, golden sky.

Ariel shed her space suit. Her once frozen heart beat wildly in her chest. As the girl looked around, she saw only light. She felt only love. There were no dragons, no fog, no darkness, no fear.

Ariel turned toward Gleeban, who had just taken off his scuba gear. Standing before her was a brilliant being of dazzling white light, whose boundariless shape shifted continuously, like flowing water. The girl noticed two points of emerald green near the top of Gleeban's head and an emanation of rose colored light in the center of his flowing form.

Ariel smiled a deep, broad smile and sang a dreamy lullaby, "I've never seen anyone like you. I feel so good just being here with you... and this place. Your world is so light, not at all like the Valley of Doom. Tell me everything."

The child overflowed with questions about this magical world without darkness. Gleeban sat her down on a moss-covered rock next to the pool of purple water. He answered her questions and sang her the story of Unity, telepathically transmitting to her a dramatic opera.

"Unity is a world that has transcended duality. Here there is no choice between good or bad, love or fear, right or wrong, darkness or light. Here there is only light... the free, clear expression of all feelings, including anger, hurt, and disappointment. We embrace all experience on Unity, even the most frightening. Here, darkness is touched by the light and transformed."

At first Ariel could not believe hear ears. "You mean I can sing as much as I want and no one will tell me to be quiet?"

"Yes, Ariel. You can sing to your heart's delight."

"How is it possible, Gleeban? How can a world like this be real?"

Gleeban explained, "Many years ago Unity was much like your Earth, Ariel. Our world was cloaked in a shroud of darkness, evil and terror. There were a few of us who dared to explore the depths of inner space. We sought answers to the basic conflicts of life. After many initiations, we discovered that fear often speaks to us in the shape of some external monster, like your Dragon King. In reality, these monsters are really a reflection of our own wrong beliefs about life. We came to understand that no matter what happens outside us, no matter how terrible or scary, we are completely safe, because darkness is an illusion. When you touch it with love, it transforms."

"If you want, Ariel, I'll bring you to the Inner Circle of Teachers, and we will teach you this miracle of transformation. Before you agree, however, you must understand that you'll need to heal yourself of all the erroneous beliefs that you cling to and agree to bring what you've learned back to your people. Now search inside. Ask your heart for an answer."

Ariel paused. Gleeban's conditions were serious. She pondered her dilemma, then searched inside and found a kernel of hope within her heart. The girl turned to her new friend and in her mind sang an energetic, enthusiastic show tune, "Yes, oh yes! I'll do anything to free my people from their fear."

Gleeban replied with a jazz riff, "Come with me, come with me, come with me, brave friend. Miracles await!"

Gleeban brought Ariel to a small hamlet of structures that might be called cottages except that they changed shape constantly just like the beings of light who inhabited them. The ET led Ariel to one of the largest of these buildings, and then into the chamber of the Inner Circle of Teachers. Gleeban introduced Ariel to the teachers and asked her to repeat the oath she had taken at the pool of imperial purple water. The Inner Circle welcomed her as an initiate.

Ariel's training began immediately. The Teachers instructed her in the art of scanning her body for fear, breathing seven deep breaths, then bringing it into her heart to be transformed. This was difficult for the girl. She believed that darkness was bad and should be avoided, not embraced.

One day Ariel was sitting on the blue grass outside the chamber of the Inner Circle, frustrated and feeling inadequate, when Gleeban sat down beside her. The ET sent her a lovely melody through his mind, "My dear friend, you are trying too hard and judging yourself mercilessly. You can't think your way through this. You have to experience the fear, not as a separate force from love, but as a distortion of love. Likewise, darkness is not the opposite of light, but a twisting of the same energy. When you touch the fear with love, instead of judging and pushing it away, it will change back into its true nature. You don't have to force anything."

The ET told Ariel to breathe deeply and allow herself to really feel her fear. He sang, "Accept yourself completely, as you are right now."

The young girl was reluctant, but she trusted Gleeban. Ariel turned toward her terror. In that instant Ariel saw the Dragon King in her mind. She raged at him, "Enough of your bullying!" Then she touched the beast tenderly with her hand. A tear trickled from the corner of his eye, then the magic monster vanished into harmlessness. Ariel smiled. Her fear had taken its rightful place in the family of things.

"Gleeban, my fear is no bigger than an insect in that great big meadow behind my cottage."

"Hmmm, hmmm," the ET hummed. "Yes, little friend. It's true. Now you've graduated to the next step."

Gleeban and the Teachers instructed her in the proper use of the healing tools of music, laughter, imagination and love. This part of the training was easy for the young girl. The Teachers simply helped her re-awaken her natural gifts.

When Ariel's education was complete, Gleeban brought her back to the Chamber of the Inner Circle. The Teachers congratulated Ariel. They spent a few moments celebrating, then silence fell upon the gathering.

The ET stood before the girl and transmitted a somber melody, "You must now return to Earth, touch the Dragon King with love and bring his dark energy of fear into the light. I'll come stand by your side. However, this is your final rite of initiation and you must go through it alone."

Ariel was saddened by the thought of leaving the wondrous world of Unity to return home, where the dragon of fear ruled. She took seven deep breaths and opened her heart. She allowed her misgivings to shoot out the top of her head and flow back down her body in a fountain of dazzling white light. Ariel turned to Gleeban and sang, "I'm ready."

Gleeban escorted Ariel back through the forest, down to the meadow, and up to the edge of the pool of imperial purple water. The young girl put on her space suit and the ET once again donned his high-tech scuba gear. With seven deep breaths and a simultaneous leap, they dove together deeper and deeper into the void of inner space, until they found themselves on the top of Dragon Mountain at the mouth of the great monster's lair.

Gleeban moved behind a rock, within a short distance, so Ariel could feel his presence. The beast's howl pierced her heart as he emerged from the darkness. "How dare you challenge the Dragon King! I'll not only destroy you, but take retribution on your village for your disrespect and brazen disregard of my power."

Ariel stood motionless. She gazed into the monster's fiery eyes and saw only her own fear reflected back to her. The girl breathed seven deep breaths, as she had been taught, allowed her heart to fill with love, then touched the beast tenderly on his snout, as orange flames and black smoke curled out his nostrils.

When she looked again, she noticed that he was just as frightened of her and the inhabitants of the village below as they were of him. The girl sang a sweet, lyrical tune. The Dragon King's eyes filled with tears. As the salty wetness trickled down his face, the beast's shape began to shift until, suddenly, the monstrous dragon became a harmless dragonfly, his iridescent wings creating tiny rainbows when the light hit them just right.

Ariel laughed out loud, "It worked... just like I imagined." The exuberant girl ran to Gleeban and hugged him (as best as anyone can hug a being of light). They laughed and sang together on top of the great mountain. As Ariel peered into the valley below, she watched the dense fog evaporate.

A brief cleansing shower passed over, then the sky opened up and the sun poured into the valley. A rainbow touched down, spreading joy from one edge of town to the other.

Ariel saw her parents, then the rest of the villagers tentatively venture out of their homes. They gathered in the center of town and held hands in a large circle. Much to her great surprise and delight the inhabitants of the once dreary valley began to chant a glorious chant of gratitude. Ariel's heart leapt.

She turned to Gleeban and transmitted this message via a tender tune, "Won't you please come home with me for a while and join the celebration?"

Gleeban looked lovingly into Ariel's eyes and sang, "Dear friend, it's time for me to go home and... it's time for you to teach the people of the valley how to touch their fear with love. Sing a song for me. And don't forget, we have a date to go diving next Tuesday at three."

They hugged once again and with a glistening moistness in her eyes, Ariel clambered down the side of the mountain toward home. The dragonfly followed along, ready to take his rightful place in the wildflower meadow, behind the clapboard cottage, at the edge of the village, nestled in what was now the Valley of Joy.

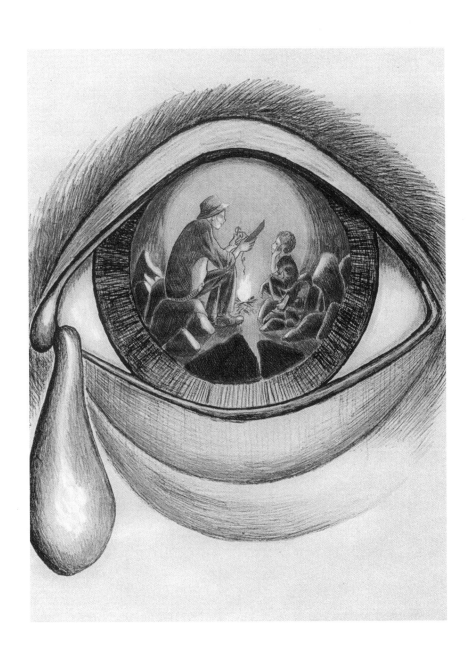

THE GOLDEN THREAD

*g*ackson fidgeted in his chair in the waiting room of his psychotherapist's office, wondering how on earth he had gotten to this point in his life. He was an intelligent, attractive, easy-going young man and it just didn't make sense to him why his world was falling apart. *My life is totally out of control,* he thought, as he pondered the last two weeks.

A week ago Saturday, his girlfriend broke their engagement. "You either don't have any feelings," she cried, as she ushered him out the door, "or you're just plain old withholding. Either way, I've had enough!"

Then, just yesterday, his boss ordered him to clear out his desk. Jackson was always daydreaming and never got his reports in on time... or so his boss said. Jackson never really noticed that he walked around in a fog at work or that he didn't express his feelings to his girlfriend.

The young man was dumbfounded. Instead of anger or regret, numbness spread through his body. He thought, *I guess I should be feeling something... but I don't.* That's when he called his therapist, Greg, and asked him what to do. Greg simply made an appointment for the distraught young man and told him he thought it might be a good idea for him to come in twice a week for a while.

Jackson stared blankly at the print of Van Gogh's, "Starry Night," hanging tilted on the flat grey wall opposite his chair. A deep despair, one he had tried hard to stave off since childhood, crept insidiously into his chest. *I'm a good guy*, he thought. *Why am I losing everything I love?*

Then he picked up his shoulders, pushed out his chest, and heard himself say, "Buck up, kid. Don't let this get you down. You don't have to feel this pain. Just tough it out." Suddenly the young man realized that his father was talking to him... only now it had become his own voice.

Then Jackson heard another voice from somewhere deep inside, this one tiny, like a child in pain, "I won't feel sad! Never! Never! Never!" Quite unexpectedly, a single tear squeaked out the corner of the young man's eye.

Jackson closed his eyes. He was startled by a sharp pain in his heart, as if someone had plunged a long, thin knife into his chest, right between his ribs. Jackson clutched his shirt, gasping for air. "God, I'm too young to have a heart attack!" He cried out, "Greg, I think I'm dying. I need your help, *now!*" Everything went blank.

A few moments later, Jackson opened his eyes and shook his head. His mouth dropped open. Instead of his therapist standing over him with an emergency medical technician nearby, paddles in hand, ready to shock him back into life, the young man was startled to find a truly ancient old man sitting in the adjacent chair.

The wizened elder sported a neatly combed beard as white as December snow. It grew down to his belly and so did the soft white hair on his head. The odd-looking character wore a deep purple cape with a hood, colorfully decorated with unusual symbols. He carried a walking stick with the head of a dragon carved into its top.

Jackson scrutinized the character for a long while until he realized the old man reminded him of a wizard in a fairy tale his grandfather used to read to him when he had trouble falling asleep as a boy. Jackson finally pulled himself together and asked the old man who he was. The seasoned old fellow replied in a craggy voice, "Let's just say, I'm a friend."

Jackson was a bit annoyed. He wasn't getting what he wanted from the old guy, so he asked again, "Who are you and why are you here... and how'd you get into this office anyway?"

The old man softened his tone, "You called, I came. I'm here to help you say goodbye to your grandfather."

Jackson was truly perplexed. He thought, *who is this guy and how'd he know I needed help... and what's this business about my grandfather?*

The young man's thoughts turned to the accident. His grandfather had died sixteen years ago. Jackson was just nine. "What are you talking about, old man?" The irritation in the young man's voice was pronounced. "I dealt with that a long time ago and I'm certainly not interested in dredging up the past. I've got enough to deal with right here and now."

The wary young man was about to dismiss the stranger when the old guy gave him a full-toothed, grin. "Whatever you say, son. I just thought you might need a friendly ear."

For no reason Jackson could explain, the armor around his heart began to melt, like the slow, soft dissolve of a chocolate ice cream cone in a warm summer breeze. He found he liked the old man, in spite of himself. Without thinking, the young man began to tell the stranger what his life had been like recently. The old man listened patiently, nodding and smiling. Jackson began to trust him.

Finally, after what seemed liked hours, Jackson asked the ancient man what he meant when he said that he was here to help him say goodbye to his grandfather. The stranger explained, "You see, son, when you were a boy you never had the opportunity to say a proper goodbye to your grandfather."

The old man pointed to Jackson's heart with his gnarled hand. "There's a sad little boy in there, that you've hidden from all these years. Now you've lost your job and you've lost your girlfriend and you don't know what to do with your feelings. Lucky for you they both had sense enough to boot you out the door, and I heard your cry for help."

Jackson's thoughts were jumbled. *Who is this weird old guy,* he mused, *and where does he get off telling me how to live my life? How can he possibly know what I'm going through.* Still... with all the doubt, there was something about the craggy old man Jackson found comforting.

The elder stared at the young man, then challenged him, "Well, what's your decision? You going to sit here forever wondering why life has dealt you such a lousy hand or come out of hiding? It's your choice."

The tears welled up in Jackson's eyes. He suddenly felt small and afraid. "Look, I don't know how... I'm scared."

The old man softened. "All you need to do, son, is close your eyes and breathe. I'll be right here with you for as long as you need me. You're really quite safe, I promise."

Jackson sighed an enormous sigh, "You promise?"
"Yes, I promise."

"Okay, old man, I asked for help. You're what I got. Let's do it."

The craggy old man, pushed himself up with his cane, stood next to Jackson and opened his cloak. Dangling from a chain over his heart was a rose quartz crystal. Jackson's eyes popped wide as the precious stone began to glow, emanating a soft pink light that seemed to fill the room.

The young man noticed a satisfying warmth spread through his body, liquefying the frozen mass he'd created around his sadness. "Okay, now," the old man instructed, "close your eyes and breathe deeply. Breathe your breath into every cell of your body."

The old man reached out gingerly, touching Jackson in the center of his chest, right below the breastbone. Before Jackson realized what was happening, he found himself, with the old man at his right shoulder, standing directly in front of his boyhood home, a three-story Victorian with a wrap-around porch.

The old man took Jackson's hand and led him up the stairs to the main entry. As the elder reached for the doorknob, Jackson stopped breathing. The old man squeezed his hand and whispered into his ear, "Breathe." The large oak door creaked open.

The two quietly entered the dwelling. They walked through Jackson's childhood living room, into the kitchen, then onto the porch. Jackson was astonished to find his grandfather sitting on the stoop, whittling a wooden whistle out of a branch from the cherry tree in the backyard. Settled beside his grandfather, gazing up with great admiration in his eyes, was a very dirty, but very happy little boy.

As Jackson approached, he recognized the boy. "That's me," he whispered to his companion. "That's me when I was nine."

Jackson's heart expanded as he watched the boy interact with his grandfather. He remembered the wonderful times together... fishing in Miller's Pond, playing catch until nightfall when his mother had to call them in from the dark... and whittling. Whittling for hour upon dreamy hour on the back porch stairs, lulled into a quiet relaxation by the constant chirp of the katydids.

Jackson also remembered the baseball games, the hotdogs and ice cream. And the fairy tales his grandfather told him when Jackson couldn't fall asleep at night.

In the next instant, Jackson's attention was drawn from this idyllic scene to a loud rapping at the front door. "It's the police, ma'am. There's been an accident." Jackson's heart contracted as he rushed into the living room and saw two uniformed patrolmen talking in whispered tones to his mother.

Then Jackson's father burst into the room. "What's going on?"

"We're sorry, sir. The driver of the truck fell asleep at the wheel, crossed over the median strip on the interstate and front-ended your father's car. There was nothing Rescue could do. Your father was gone by the time they arrived."

Without saying a word, Jackson's father turned his back on the men. He walked straight for the liquor cabinet and furiously grabbed a bottle of whiskey.

Jackson's mother held back her tears, restraining her sorrow against the advent of a reprisal from her soon to be intoxicated husband. She turned her vacant gaze back towards the navy blue uniforms, standing stiffly on the front steps, hardly noticing the drawn faces of the men who wore them. "Thank you, officers." Jackson's mother quietly closed the door and walked silently up the stairs to her bedroom.

Jackson watched this scene with the same empty horror he'd felt as a child. "Grandpa," he blurted out. Then the flood of tears came.

Without warning, Jackson felt the back of his father's hand across his face. "Stop crying!" the drunken man seethed. "Be a man... as if I didn't have enough to worry about without having to take care of a crybaby."

Jackson heard that small voice deep within him scream, "Then I won't feel sad. I'll never feel sad again. NEVER! NEVER! NEVER!"

Jackson re-experienced the tightening of his jaw, the reddening of his face, the wrenching of his stomach and the shear humiliation of his father's rejection in the face of such a tragic loss. The frozen mass began to re-form around his heart.

Jackson turned to his ancient companion who was still holding his hand. "I feel like I'm going to die. I'm not sure I can tolerate this pain, but I *am* sure I can't keep recreating this scene over and over again in my life. I have to stop freezing up whenever I feel sad. Please, help me say goodbye to my grandfather."

The old man escorted Jackson back to where the little boy was still intently watching his grandfather whittle. "Jackson," the elder instructed, "go sit next to the boy and take him in your arms."

Jackson embraced the little boy, cradling him tenderly next to his chest. Suddenly, the boy melted into the young man's frame. Reunited with himself, Jackson felt truly alive for the first time since the day his grandfather had died.

"Now, tell your grandfather everything you wanted to tell him but never had the chance."

Jackson slipped his hand into his grandfather's, looked into his sparkling eyes and said in the voice of a nine year old, "Grampa, I'm really mad that you died. I think my heart's broken, I miss you so much. I really, really love you, and I wish you hadn't died."

Jackson sobbed. With the torrent unleashed, his upper body rocked involuntarily to uncontested waves of grief. His thoughts flashed first to his girlfriend, then to his last day at work, and then back to his grandfather.

Jackson reached out, hugged his grandfather and through disjointed breaths said, "Goodbye, Grampa. I'll never forget you."

Jackson's grandfather smiled and without a word returned the young man's embrace. Then his image vanished into thin air.

In the next instant, Jackson found himself back in the waiting room of his therapist's office. The wizened old man still had his hand on the center of Jackson's chest. Jackson felt sad, but the deep despair and the profound ache in his heart had disappeared. He smiled at the elder and took a deep breath.

Then, for the first time, Jackson gazed intently into the stranger's eyes. Jackson leapt out of his chair and roared with delight, "Grampa, it's you! Why didn't you tell me?"

"Now really, Jackson. If I'd told you, would you have believed me?"

Jackson scratched his head and remarked, "You know, it is kind of hard. I don't exactly believe in ghosts. At least, not before today"

The old man replied, "Well, I'm not exactly a ghost. But I have been watching over you from the world of spirit. You see, son, death is really just a transition from one dimension of life to another. We've always been connected to each other, heart to heart, by a golden thread of love that can never be diminished, even by separation or death."

"When you decided to stop feeling, you momentarily cut off that connection. It's your missing me, your longing, that brings us closer together. I've always been with you and I've always loved you."

Jackson squeezed his grandfather's hand tightly. His grandfather squeezed back and said, "I have to go now, son... remember the golden thread of love."

The old man instructed the young man to sit quietly in his chair. "Now close your eyes again and breathe deeply." Jackson sensed the tender touch of his grandfather's hand on his heart. A warm radiance of love permeated his body.

In the next instant, Jackson was startled into opening his eyes by the concerned hand of his therapist on his shoulder, shaking him lightly. "Jack, it's time for your session. You must have fallen asleep while you were waiting for me."

Jackson was a bit dazed. He mumbled under his breath, "Was it a dream? Have I really been asleep." Then he remembered the golden thread. He imagined a soft, velvet cord spiraling up from his heart to the heavens and felt the warm touch of love from his grandfather's hand flowing back down toward his heart. "No. It wasn't a dream."

Greg looked quizzically at his bleary-eyed client, "Did you say something about a dream, Jack? Is that what you wanted to talk about today?"

Jackson stood up abruptly, grabbed his jacket from the back of the chair and shouted to Greg as he ran out the door, "Sorry about the appointment. I have to visit my grandfather's grave. Then I'm going to a ball game. Then I'm going to call my girlfriend. I'll see you next week."

As Jackson ran down the steps of the old brownstone office building, he noticed the warmth of the sun on the back of his neck. He turned his eyes upward and spotted a passing cloud. He laughed. It resembled an old man with sparkling eyes and a long white beard.

The young man gave a quick wave and shouted into the brilliant blue sky, "Don't worry, Grampa, I won't forget." Then he ambled down the street, tasting the bitter-sweetness of longing on his tongue... touched by the golden thread of love.

ELIZABETH AND THE UNICORN

ons ago in a tiny hamlet, nestled in a glen not far from the edge of forever, lived a beautiful little girl named Elizabeth. Elizabeth dwelled in a small cottage by a large oak tree with her father and step-mother, step-brother and twin sister. Elizabeth was not a happy child for she was trying very hard to grow up in a family that was very hard to grow up in.

Her family loved her, but had a very strange way of showing it. Whenever anyone touched the little girl, it hurt.

Elizabeth's step-mother insisted that she wash her in the wooden tub, even though Elizabeth was old enough to bathe herself. When her step-mother first placed her in the tub, Elizabeth enjoyed the sensation of the warm soapy water gently flowing down her back. But then the compulsive woman scrubbed her all over with a hard bristle brush until her skin turned red, screaming, "I must be certain every nook and cranny of your body is clean, otherwise you'll embarrass me in public."

Every night Elizabeth's father came to her room, sat at the foot of the bed and read her a story. She felt comforted by the physical presence of her father and the melodic sound of his voice. After he finished the story, however, he'd grab her tightly and squeeze her so hard she felt like her lungs would collapse. Elizabeth hated his hugs, but he seemed to need it. And the good little girl didn't want to disappoint her father, who'd suffered many disappointments in life.

Often, when the weather was good, her older step-brother would play with Elizabeth near the old oak tree. At first he'd pretend to be a butterfly and let her chase him. She relished the sensation of her footfalls on the soft, brown earth and the gentle touch of the breeze on her bare skin. The older boy often let her catch him. But then, the much larger and stronger boy would turn on her, suddenly pretending to be a giant grizzly bear. He'd grab her harshly, hold her upside down by her feet, swing her around and around, then drop her down hard on the ground. The bully would laugh as the little girl with skinned knees and bruised arms made a desperate dash for the cottage.

Instead of comforting Elizabeth and admonishing her son, Elizabeth's step-mother would invariably confront the disheveled child at the doorway. "Look at you!" the frenzied woman shrieked. "You're covered in filth. You belong in the pig sty." Then she'd force the baffled girl to strip off her clothes in front of everyone and banish her to her room. The step-mother shunned Elizabeth for days, forbidding anyone to touch her. "Don't you touch that wicked girl," she'd wail, "or you'll catch some dreadful disease, maybe even the plague!"

Soon Elizabeth began to believe that, indeed, she was wicked. Even more insidious was the thought that maybe it was the pleasure she felt when the warm soapy water trickled down her back, or her delight in the soothing baritone of her father's voice, or the whispered touch of the breeze on her bare skin that made her family respond with harsh, confusing touch or no touch at all. *It's my fault,* she thought. *My step-mother's right. I'm a wicked girl and my body is very bad. I'm just not lovable.*

In spite of everything, however, the wounded child loved her family. *If I could just make my body do what I want and not feel good at the wrong times,* she thought, *then maybe they'll stop hurting me.*

Elizabeth soon noticed she could tighten her body and hold her breath when she first stepped into the tub, or heard her father's voice or felt the breeze on her bare skin. Then she wouldn't feel pleasure in her body. Unfortunately, the more she tightened, the stiffer she became until she was so tight that she couldn't move at all, her body a contorted gnarl.

Elizabeth refused to eat or run or play or move or do anything that might bring her enjoyment. The misguided child was convinced that it was the "wicked" pleasure she desired that made others touch her so harshly.

Soon Elizabeth forgot she had a body. She stayed in her room for long periods of time, curled into a tiny ball on her bed, barely breathing, dreaming that one day some kind soul would rescue her... But no one came. A terrible hopelessness crept into her knotted muscles.

One day Elizabeth's twin sister charged into the bedroom, arms flailing, screaming at the top of her lungs. The frenzied girl hit her bewildered sister without mercy. "Step-mother says you're wicked. You make her so mad. Why don't you just go away! She says we'd all be better off."

This was the last straw. Without thinking, Elizabeth let loose a tremendous blow to the back of her twin's head, knocking her to the floor, unconscious.

Elizabeth cried, "Oh no!" The young girl, realizing she had lost herself in her rage, raced out of the cottage. Her tears burned like hot acid, etching deep lines of remorse into her face. She ran past the oak tree and down the path that wound its way through the glen, then up into the rolling hills overlooking the vale.

As Elizabeth fled, she vowed never to return to her family. In that instant she decided unequivocally, *I'm never going to touch anyone again. And I'm never, ever going to let anyone touch me!*

Elizabeth was soon gasping for breath. She stumbled up a hill, then collapsed underneath a large lilac bush. The sweet fragrance of the flowering shrub was exquisite, but she refused to allow herself the pleasure of even one brief whiff.

The exhausted girl noticed a few tears trying to force themselves out through her hardened eyes, but she shook her head quickly, shut her eyes tightly and with great determination in her voice said, "No. I won't feel this. I won't think about what happened. I'm just going to lie here under this bush and die."

In spite of herself, the little girl could not help smelling the tantalizing, watery fragrance of the tiny lavender buds that were now blossoming into cone-shaped wonders. She opened her eyes to get a better look, curious about the simple pleasure that was drawing her attention away from the knot in her stomach.

When Elizabeth looked up, she was startled to see a stunning, white Unicorn with deep azure eyes gazing down at her with great tenderness. The Unicorn had an impressive spiral horn, telescoping out from the middle of his forehead and wore multi-colored ribbons streaming from a long flowing mane. The sleek animal seemed to shimmer in the late afternoon sun.

"Hello, Dear One." The Unicorn smiled as he tenderly nuzzled the little girl with his long, slender nose. "What, may I ask, are you doing on the path so far from the hamlet?"

Elizabeth was startled, quickly retreating from the Unicorn. "Don't touch me!" the little girl snarled, as if she were a tigress backed into the corner of a small cage.

The Unicorn looked perplexed, then replied with a hint of understanding in his voice, "But of course, my dear, I respect your desire not to be touched. Although I have to say, it saddens me deeply that you do not wish to partake of this delightful pleasure."

Elizabeth was moved by the Unicorn's willingness to respect her boundaries. For a moment, the defensive little girl noticed a hint of hope gurgling up from her belly. She thought, *maybe, just maybe I can trust him.*

As if the sky had opened up, the forlorn little girl deluged the shimmering white beast with her sad and painful story. "And it was then," Elizabeth finished, "I decided never to touch anyone or let them touch me, ever again."

The Unicorn wept for the beautiful child's pain. "Dear One," the Unicorn sighed, "you have suffered so much in such a short life. Won't you come with me to a magical place where you might find some healing for your deep pain?"

At first Elizabeth was skeptical. She wanted to know all about this magical place the Unicorn described. "Will I have to touch people or let them touch me? Will I be hurt? Will people make me eat and play and move around?"

The questions were endless. The Unicorn listened patiently, then remarked, "The first lesson on this journey, Dear One, is that you cannot control others or what issues forth from the universe according to its natural laws. However, I understand your fears. If you believe in me and allow me to guide you further down the path, you will soon discover that you are safe and you are loved."

With these words Elizabeth noticed the knot in her stomach slowly dissolving. In the next moment the little girl stood up sharply, turned to her new companion and said, "Let's go, I'm getting hungry!"

The Unicorn guided their direction on the winding path, over the hilly terrain, through another valley, to the edge of a dense grove of giant redwood trees. Elizabeth stood still, stunned by their grandeur, craning her neck to see the top of even the smallest of the redwoods.

As the travelers entered the forest, the Unicorn turned to Elizabeth and spoke with great reverence, "These trees, Dear One, are the oldest living beings in the world. Open your heart to them. Let them touch you with their wisdom. They have many secrets to share, if you simply pay close attention."

Elizabeth held her breath. "I don't want anyone or anything to touch me."

In the next instant, a whispered breeze rustled the dense foliage of a handsome young tree, then drifted down, tenderly caressing Elizabeth's cheek. She giggled, then waited tensely for a harsh attack, ready to stiffen her body at the slightest provocation. When nothing happened, the little girl breathed a sigh of relief, gazed at the swaying giant, then opened ever so slightly to new possibilities.

They arrived at a clearing in the middle of which was a carefully laid circle of stones with an enormous fire ablaze in its center. As the Unicorn approached, a tall, slender figure with long, golden, flowing hair and blue eyes (not unlike the Unicorn's) emerged from the trunk of one of the largest redwoods.

The Unicorn introduced Elizabeth to Elcon, Queen of the Wood Nymphs. Elcon did not say a word as she held her hands, palm up, gingerly approaching the apprehensive girl. The Unicorn explained, "Elcon is welcoming you to the forest."

Elizabeth turned to her companion with a puzzled look, "I don't understand. She didn't say anything to me."

"That's because," the Unicorn replied, "long ago the Wood Nymphs gave up their sight, their hearing and their ability to speak in favor of sensing the world through touch. The Wood Nymphs live inside these wise old trees. They are able to move about quite effortlessly and communicate with others using only their sense of touch. They use their bodies to see, hear and sense the energy around them. They would like to teach you the real value of touch... if you're willing."

Elizabeth stared, with eyes wide open, at the Queen. Then the little girl sensed the Wood Nymph asking permission to touch her with her hand. At first, Elizabeth rejected the offer, "No, don't come any closer." The Queen stopped and waited.

When the little girl realized that she was in charge and that the Queen respected her "No," Elizabeth sighed. The tension in her muscles dissolved. The little girl gestured to the Wood Nymph to come closer, then gave Elcon permission to touch her.

The Queen placed her hand carefully on Elizabeth's heart. The little girl recoiled slightly, then sensed Elcon's intention not to hurt her. Slowly, but surely, Elizabeth began to feel safe and nurtured, just as the Unicorn had promised.

Without knowing why, a profound longing to be held exploded into Elizabeth's awareness. The little girl reached out. The Wood Nymph cradled the child in her slender arms, rocking her ever so slowly. Elizabeth's body melted into the Queen's embrace, her breath flowing naturally, like the quiet purr of a kitten nestled into her mother's belly.

Elizabeth heaved deep sobs of release and in the tiniest of voices squeaked, "For me? Just for me? You'll hold me just for me?"

Elcon nodded, "For as long as you want."

Elizabeth was no longer surprised she could understand the gentle thoughts of the Queen through her gestures.

Then a miracle occurred. Elizabeth noticed a faint, but definitely discernable sensation of pleasure in her little left toe. The pleasure migrated into her little right toe, then into her feet, up her legs, through her body and into her heart. In that moment, a soft pink light surrounded the entwined pair. Elizabeth felt a warm glow of love all over her body.

Elizabeth turned to the Unicorn (who'd watched this scene with a tear in his eye and a tender smile on his lips) and gave the glorious beast a big hug. The radiant child cried, "Thank you. Thank you for bringing me here!"

The Unicorn nuzzled Elizabeth, "There's much more to learn from the Wood Nymphs, Dear One. I'm going to leave you here for a while. Elcon will teach you their ancient wisdom. When you're ready to go home, I'll return and be your guide once more."

Elizabeth said goodbye, trusting that the Unicorn would reappear as promised. Then Elcon gently reached for the girl's hand and led her down a well-worn footpath to a handsome old redwood that would be her new home.

In the days that followed, the enchanted Queen tutored the girl in the marvels of touch and how to listen with her whole body. Elizabeth practiced touching with permission and allowing herself to be touched. Elizabeth was a quick study. As she learned to listen deeply, the girl was able to touch the essence of the other Wood Nymphs, and the trees and the forest animals, with love, just as she had been touched by Elcon. Soon she was no longer frightened by pleasure. With the help of the Queen, the little girl realized that her pleasurable feelings did not cause her family to hurt her, but that her family just didn't know how to touch without hurting.

Elizabeth overflowed with joy when she received, in her heart, this message from the gentle touch of the Queen, "Pleasure is our birthright. Experiencing it brings us into deep relationship with all that is sacred. Elizabeth, dear child, you deserve to feel pleasure in your body. You have a right to be touched with respect."

After Elcon was satisfied that Elizabeth could create and honor her own boundaries and teach others what she'd learned, the Queen called her to the circle of stones. There, around the blazing fire, the Wood Nymphs honored their beloved adopted daughter. Elcon presented Elizabeth with a small piece of the great redwood that had been her home, as a reminder of all she had learned from the spirits of those wise and venerable woods.

Elizabeth wept softly. She asked permission, then slowly and lovingly cradled each of the Wood Nymphs in her arms to say farewell.

When she approached Elcon, the radiant child reached out one last time and fell into the waiting arms of her mentor. Elcon indicated, with a tender stroke on the girl's cheek, that Elizabeth now lived in their hearts and was welcome to return to the great forest any time she desired. Elizabeth took a deep breath, sighed and said goodbye. Then the Wood Nymphs vanished silently into the trees, like the remnants of a dream dissolving into the yawn of a waking child, and there, standing before the astonished girl, as promised, was the splendid Unicorn.

Elizabeth opened her arms. The Unicorn nuzzled in, then looked lovingly into her eyes and said in a sweet and gentle voice, "You've learned much. Your touch is warm and loving, and your heart is full and alive. I'm honored to be your guide once more, this time on your journey home."

With that, the beaming child tenderly caressed the side of her guide's neck. The Unicorn led his beloved Elizabeth down the winding footpath through the forest, over the hills and into the glen that was not far from the edge of forever.

THE BEAUTIFUL DIVINE BLOB

*J*onah, a handsome, articulate youth, dreamed of adventures and far away places. He lived with his family on a farm roughly two miles outside of Puritanville, a village so plain you'd hardly notice it if you walked by. The perfectly square, dust brown, frame houses and shops blended easily into the drab landscape. There were no frills on the women's dresses and nothing fancy about the men's haircuts. According to Jonah, life was altogether monotonous. Nothing out of the ordinary ever happened in Puritanville.

Jonah loved his family, but longed to travel to exotic places and meet new people. During his spare time, the youth avidly consumed volumes of mythology, wondrous tales of fantasy and adventure. His favorite story was a legend about a magical beast from another world known as the Wildling. This creature, a free spirit, appeared and disappeared anywhere he wanted, giving the beast tremendous mobility and freedom.

Jonah coveted the Wildling's abilities. He desperately wanted to transport himself out of his dreary existence. Unfortunately, his father needed the young man's help with the farm, and his mother depended on him to care for the younger children. In spite of his youthful craving for adventure, Jonah felt a strong sense of responsibility and devotion to his family.

Puritanville lived by a strict moral code. They believed in a severe and punishing God who ruled on high and watched over them as a stern father would watch over his children. Even though the rules were strict and their belief in God unyielding, love and a sense of fairness motivated each and every member of that small community.

Jonah didn't know what he believed yet. He had plenty of time to decide. One thing he understood, beyond even the slightest doubt, however, was that life was no longer simply dreary, but grew overwhelmingly desolate when the new preacher came to town. Suddenly the communal standards of love and fair play disappeared. They were replaced by fear, harsh judgement, and punishment dispensed to anyone who did not adhere perfectly to the rules forced on them by the preacher.

The preacher, de facto leader of the Church's Board of Overseers, stormed around board meetings with fire in his eyes, shaking his fists, and warning the others that their obedience to God's law was deficient. "You and your families will surely be doomed to an eternity of unspeakable torture if you do not heed my words... for I am the appointed messenger of God." Afterwards, the overseers would comply with the preacher's demand for more rules and swifter punishment of offenders.

Jonah heard about the meetings from his father, who'd return from these ordeals exhausted. One night the broken man stumbled into the old farmhouse, slumped into a straight-backed wooden chair, and wept tears of despair. "Jonah," the beleaguered man turned to his son for consolation, "I don't know what to do. I can't believe God is that cruel, but the preacher *is* the Lord's emissary and I must respect his authority."

Jonah bit his tongue, but couldn't hold back, "Father, I hate that self-righteous, pompous preacher. Look what he's done to you. Look what he's doing to the village. He's wrong, Father. I refuse to believe that God is harsh and punishing. I'm not afraid of the preacher and I'm going to tell him what I think!"

"Oh no, son," Jonah could hear the tremble in his father's voice. "You mustn't do that. God will punish you. Please, Jonah, promise me you'll keep still."

Jonah was torn between his rage at the injustice he perceived and his loyalty to his father. The young man looked down at his feet, eyes half shut, then mumbled, "I promise."

That Sunday Jonah's father was overcome, his exhausted body crushed by the weight of inner turmoil. This respected member of the community vomited in back of the barn and went directly to bed. The youth found him there, with the covers pulled up close around his ears and Jonah's mother patting his forehead with a cold compress. The weakened man coughed, staring bleary-eyed at his son, "Jonah, it's up to you today. Take your mother and the children into town for the morning call to worship. And please... remember your promise."

Jonah felt helpless in the face of his father's fear. He wanted to stay and take care of him, but knew there was nothing he could do. Besides... his father was counting on him.

The young man hitched their strongest team of horses to the heavy wagon. Jonah's brothers and sisters piled in back, dressed in their Sunday best. Mother, who sat up front with Jonah, demanded silence.

As the youth prodded the horses forward, his mother turned swiftly, sternly scrutinizing her brood. "I want you all to be on your best behavior," she snapped.

"Don't make the preacher mad! Don't disgrace your father!" As the family approached the plain, brown church at the edge of town she added, "Now bow your heads and pray to the Almighty that we be spared His terrible wrath."

Jonah was thankful he was driving so he didn't have to bow his head. He wished he could vanish, like the Wildling and re-materialize in some far away land, where singing and dancing were allowed and life was a grand adventure. But nothing like that ever happened in Puritanville.

Jonah's fury was awakened as the family sat glued stiffly to their pew at the front of the church, listening to the preacher's sermon. The foreboding figure painted a cruel picture of God with his words. "You are simple-minded, errant children to Him," the preacher admonished. Then he raised his fist into the air and smashed it down hard on the pulpit. "The Lord casts His eyes down upon you with disdain because you are unworthy sinners. You will burn for eternity in the fires of perdition if you do not repent. I say to you now, abide by His laws, delivered through me, His one and only servant and true messenger!"

In the next instant, the youngest children in the congregation began to blubber uncontrollably. Jonah heard his baby sister cry, "Mommy, I'm scared!"

The youth stood up sharply from the straight-backed wooden pew and in front of the entire assembly shouted, "What happened to the love and sense of justice in this community? All I feel now is fear. Don't believe the ravings of this madman. God isn't out to punish you. He loves you all."

Jonah was astounded by the words that blurted out of his mouth. He wasn't even sure he believed in God, but his anger had risen to a fever pitch. The young man felt compelled to speak out, to stop the preacher's reign of terror in his town.

The congregation let out a collective gasp. Then a stunned silence enveloped the hall. No one knew quite how to react or what to do. In the next moment, muffled expressions of encouragement emanated from a few members of the congregation. The preacher noticed the change in atmosphere and quickly moved to regain control. "You impious young fool, how dare you challenge my authority? I am the only true messenger of God. I speak His truth, and His word is law!"

With that, the preacher instructed several large men to seize Jonah and drag him out of the church. The youth's mother rushed up to the intimidating clergyman and knelt down, clasping her hands in a sign of prayer, "Please, sir, let him go. Forgive him, he's just a boy. He doesn't know what he's saying."

The preacher gazed at the bent figure with contempt in his eyes, "Madam, your son has visited a great shame upon your family. If I do not deal with this now, you will all suffer unspeakable pain for eternity."

The youngest children started to wail again. The preacher shoved Jonah's mother aside and quickly followed the men, who'd dragged the youth out the door by his heels, to the rear of the adjacent rectory.

There, the preacher's henchmen whipped the boy viciously as the clergyman read verses from the Holy Book. Then they hurled him into a dilapidated tool shed and locked the door. The preacher yelled through the rough wooden slats, "Let us see if this teaches you a lesson, heathen. I might let you out, if and when you fall on your knees and apologize to me for your impertinence." The pompous preacher stormed away.

It took a moment for Jonah to find his bearings. The shed had no windows. The only visible light was a faint shaft, edging its way through a narrow crack just above the solid dirt floor, between two rough wooden wall boards.

The youth was bruised and scraped. Fatigue quickly overwhelmed him. He worried about what would happen to his family as a result of his outburst. *That lunatic is gong to shun them, too,* he thought. The young man didn't mind so much for himself, but he knew that a rejection like that would destroy his family, especially his father.

A searing pain shot through Jonah's chest. For a brief moment, the young man considered the possibility of crawling to the preacher on bended knee to ask forgiveness... if only to relieve his family's torment. *That won't do any good,* he thought, realizing that his action would offer only a temporary resolution to a much greater dilemma, the preacher's tyranny over the town. *There has to be another way,* the youth puzzled, *but what?*

As he contemplated his difficulty, Jonah noticed the tiny crack of light in the wall expand into a doorway large enough for a horse to pass through. A shaft of brilliant white light radiated through the opening. Before the young man could blink, a strange and wondrous beast ambled into the shed. Jonah was stunned. "Wow! Nothing like this ever happens in Puritanville!"

Long, golden hair covered the animal's body. He was muscular in build, but agile and graceful in his gait. He looked a bit like a cross between a thoroughbred stallion and a gazelle, with two slender horns attached to the crown of his head.

As he gazed into the lustrous eyes of this remarkable beast, Jonah sensed courage, wisdom and love. The creature smiled and with slight amusement in his voice said, "So, I guess you're wondering who I am?"

Without hesitation Jonah replied, "I know who you are. You're the Wildling from my favorite story!"

The beast was delighted by the youth's recognition. "Yes, my young friend. My name is Feral. I've been keeping my eye on you and noticed your predicament. How can I help?"

Relieved, Jonah took a deep breath and focused on his heart's longing. A moment later he said, "It's not just about getting me out of this shed. I need to find out about the true nature of God. Then I know I can convince the community that there's nothing to fear. Love and fairness would come back to the valley."

The Wildling's eyes sparkled, "You're very bright, Jonah... and you have a noble intention. I think I can help you in your quest for the truth."

Jonah's eyes lit up. "Yes!" he shouted. "Let's get started."

The Wildling instructed Jonah to get on his back. Together they walked into the shaft of light, through the crack in the wall and re-materialized in another world, vibrant and teeming with life. Vital shafts of light radiated from three different suns in the sky. Rainbows dotted the horizon. Jonah was not prepared for what he saw. "We're not in Puritanville anymore, are we?"

The Wildling chortled, "No, we're not."

Jonah's heart overflowed with joy as he dismounted the Wildling. The youth noticed a growing sense of freedom that he had never experienced before. Jonah turned to the Wildling and asked, "Where are we?"

Feral replied, "The Source. This is where all life begins. We've come to join a pilgrimage to the fountain at the center. That's the doorway to the cycle of life, death, and rebirth. It's the only way to know the true nature of God."

"I'm not sure I like the part about death, Feral."

"Don't worry, my young friend, dying is quite an adventure. You're completely safe and I'll be right by your side."

With that, the interdimensional travelers set off down the path toward the center of the Source. As they walked, others joined them. Jonah was astonished to see a pod of spotted dolphins and another pod of humpback whales swim past them on their way to the fountain. Then he spied a ginger-colored kitten trailing after a young woman and an old man carrying a infant girl gingerly in his arms. He also saw ferocious mythical monsters, dragons and other shadowy creatures. Much to his amazement, Jonah also observed spirits of long dead relatives, angels and additional otherworldly entities marching with single-minded purpose to the center of the Source.

After a long while, that transpired in a flash, the pilgrims entered a clearing. In its center was a bottomless pool of bluish green water. From the core sprang an exquisite fountain of light spraying starbursts of rainbow color into the azure sky. A surge of pleasure flooded every cell of the young man's body. Jonah laughed out loud.

In the next moment, the Wildling, Jonah, and the other pilgrims formed a circle around the fountainhead and clasped hands. Suddenly everyone in attendance merged into a unified whole. Initially, the young man was frightened, but slowly opened himself to the pleasure of fellowship as he joined with the beasts, the birds, the bugs, the humans, spirits and angels, becoming one with this beautiful Blob of Divine Consciousness, never losing his individuality, his unique ray in the spectrum of light.

Then the Divine Blob embraced the stones, the trees, the clouds, the air, the suns and the very earth upon which it rested. The growing entity shifted and moved in a constant state of flux... always and forever creating and recreating itself into new forms and higher levels of awareness.

Suddenly the young man noticed a deep purple cloud lurking just outside the awareness of this fluid divine consciousness. A shadowy figure emerged from the haze and tried to infuse the Blob with a scarlet vapor of hatred. The young man recoiled as the gaseous stream made its way toward him. Jonah's fear abated quickly as the evil vapor was enveloped by the totality of the Blob.

Jonah turned to the Wildling for an explanation. "What was that?"

Feral answered the youth in a somber tone, "The Source created all sentient beings with free will. Unfortunately, the shadow coveted power and wanted to rule over a kingdom of his own, so a long time ago, he chose to leave the beautiful Blob."

The Wildling continued, "The longer he stays separate, the more fragmented and negative he becomes. The purpose of the pilgrimage is to invite the shadow figure back into the Blob. Until the day he willingly returns, this divine consciousness will not be fulfilled."

In the next moment, the Blob turned toward the figure at the edge of its boundary and reached out to the unreconciled element of creation. He refused, once again, turning his back on the fellowship. Realizing he was powerless over the Blob, he skulked away.

Jonah experienced an overwhelming sense of loss. Feral, "That was incredibly sad. But I don't understand something. You said you would help me find the true nature of God. Who is God and what does God have to do with the shadow?"

The Wildling handed Jonah a mirror and said, "Look. Behold the face of God."

Jonah gazed into the glass but saw only his own reflection. "But I'm not God. How can this be?"

Feral replied, "Look again."

As Jonah peered into the reflecting glass once more, he was astonished to watch his face melt into the face of the old man who carried the infant down the path. Then it dissolved into the face of the baby, the likeness of the young woman with the kitten, a spotted dolphin, an angel, and the fountain itself. Each image swirled and dissolved into the next, until finally, the young man recognized the face of the shadow figure.

An overpowering impulse to turn away came over him. Jonah jerked back his hand, almost losing the mirror... But an even more powerful force drew his eyes back to the reflection.

"Oh, my God," he cried. "It's the preacher!"

"Reach out, Jonah," the Wildling urged, "reach out with your heart. See him through the compassionate eyes of God."

Jonah noticed the fear in the preacher's wide-eyed gaze. Then a longing emerged from the young man's soul. A desire so strong, it moved his trembling hand toward the mirror. As Jonah touched the preacher, a fierce fire consumed his image, and Jonah reappeared in the glass, joined again with the Divine Blob.

With his eyes full of wonder and a thousand questions on his lips, Jonah turned to the Wildling, "How can this be? I was taught that God is some stern authority who sits up in heaven and punishes us when we're bad."

The Wildling looked lovingly into Jonah's eyes and replied, "God is inside of you and you are part of this beautiful Blob of Divine Consciousness. The true nature of God is all that you've just experienced, eternal creative energy. You are the embodiment of that energy and so is the preacher. We are all splashes in this sparkling fountain of life, each a different color of the rainbow."

In the next instant, Jonah experienced an energy surge in his body. The young man's uncertainty about God died, in that moment, and he was reborn into a new consciousness of boundless love and an unshakable faith in his own divinity.

The youth turned to his wise and trusted friend, with one last question, "What about the preacher? He's evil. What do I do about the preacher?"

Feral gazed intently at the young man and replied, "Evil is born from a deep-seated fear of belonging. The preacher is afraid he'll be consumed by the fire of love if he rejoins the Blob, so he uses fear and intimidation to keep himself separate. But as you experienced, Jonah, you didn't lose yourself in the Blob, you simply merged with a greater reality."

The Wildling continued, "Your path, my friend, is to embrace and transform the shadowy reflection of the preacher inside you. Only then will you be able to bring this wisdom to your community. But remember, Jonah, you must touch the preacher with love, not judgement. See him through the eyes of God. If you try to control him, you will only increase his power."

"I understand." Then the young man mused, "You know, Feral, I never would've guessed that I'd find God inside of me!"

The Wildling nuzzled the youth with his broad, flat nose and laughed, "Well, you know, my young friend, you're not in Puritanville anymore!"

Jonah allowed himself one more moment of merging with the fullness of the beautiful Blob, then he mounted the Wildling. In a flash, the enchanted beast transported the young man back to the unlit tool shed.

Before the Wildling departed, Jonah gave him an enormous hug. Feral smiled and said, "Jonah, remember the Blob... Remember who you are. Now go and teach the others what you've learned about the nature of God. You must lead, even if no one follows and teach, even if no one listens. This is your path."

With that, the beautiful beast disappeared through the crack in the wall. Suddenly, the door flew open. The young man was immediately confronted by the preacher and his henchmen. Jonah met the clergyman's stern gaze with love, then walked out of the dark shed into the world with an unshakable faith in his own divinity and a deep understanding of the true nature of God.

THE RAINBOW WARRIOR WOMAN

unete was an exceptional girl. At the age of eleven she could out-run, out-jump, and out-dance every other child in the Noble Janqua Clan. She was exceedingly bright and always raised a smile on the face of anyone she met. Some believed it was her charm that touched such joy in others. But the elders of the Clan saw something else in the girl, underneath her engaging exterior, deep within her core. They could see it in the deep pool of her soft brown eyes, the gateway to her soul. They saw a brilliance that could not be outdone by the blazing white fire of the North Star against the black canvas of the midnight sky.

The elders knew, deep in their hearts, that Hunete was the child who would carry the teachings of the Noble Clan into the world during the time of great changes on their home world, Ordinon, the twelfth planet in the twelfth ring around Argaelia.

The prophesy was revealed to the Council of Elders long ago, during the full moon ceremony on the twelfth night, of the twelfth month, of the twelfth cycle of Ordinon. The Council gathered around the central fire when Eagle Spirit, the shaman of the Noble Clan, fell into a trance and uttered these words, "In twelve generations, when the cycles repeat themselves, a child among you who has suffered greatly, will step forward to become the light bearer of the Noble Janqua Clan, first tribe of the

Rainbow Warrior People. She will end the discord amongst all beings on this planet and usher in the Eternal Reign of Peace."

As the time of the twelve cycles approached, the elders were motivated by a growing urgency about their appointed task. They were to complete Hunete's training and prepare the girl for her initiation as the light bearer of the Clan. Until then she would be incapable of assuming her essential role in the spiritual growth of the planet. To the Noble Clan, Ordinon was a living, breathing being, and their wellness was inextricably bound to her wellness. The child's rite of ascension was of immense importance.

Hunete appeared to be a strong, free-spirited child. However, beneath the surface lurked a gnawing sense of insecurity and a powerful hunger for control, born from the womb of tragedy.

Little was known of Hunete's mother, who died in childbirth. The girl's father spent the next several years of his life consuming enormous quantities of fire brew, trying to escape from his pain. He often snarled at Hunete, blaming her for the death of his beloved mate. One night he got so drunk he beat his little girl with one of her mother's old beaded belts, raising welts on her back as red as hot coals. Without a word, the grief-stricken man fled into the desert. Hunete never saw her father again.

Hunete's Grandmother and Grandfather raised her. They loved her deeply and tried to make up for their son's disgrace with kindness. But nothing could ever make up for the child's loss.

The Elders observed Hunete carefully. As the time of initiation approached, their anxiety increased. They knew full well that her physical and mental abilities were exceptional. However, the girl's willful pride, which masked her insecurity, hindered her growth. She was blocked from fully utilizing her talents, and thus unable to share her gifts with the world.

Hunete constantly bragged to the other children and bullied them into doing things her way. When afraid she wouldn't excel at some game or didn't understand how to play it, she changed the rules. These tactics ensured Hunete's victory in any competition she entered. However, soon none of the children wanted to play with her.

The boastful girl was also disrespectful of her elders. She often argued with them, even though she didn't know the right answer to their questions. She would not tolerate mistakes made by herself or others. Because Hunete was still a child, and knowing she had suffered, the elders were lenient with her. However, they also realized that the prideful girl must accept her imperfections and limitations, as well as her talents, if she were to mature into the light bearer for the Noble Clan. As Eagle Spirit had taught the elders generations ago, "Humility is an essential aspect of nobility."

With these concerns in mind, the Council of Elders convened that night. Bathed by the milky white light of the full moon, they discussed the prophesy and the completion of Hunete's training. Hunete's Grandfather, a respected member of the Council, stood before the women and men of the assembly and spoke clearly, commanding their undivided attention, "Our plan must be clever, otherwise the child will try to manipulate the circumstances. The initiation must be exciting and challenging for Hunete."

The Elders stood in a circle around the Council fire. Without a word, the assembly turned toward the north, raised their hands to the sky, palm up and prayed for the wisdom of Spirit to enter their sacred space. Then Grandmother Earth Fire, who had assumed the role of Council leader that night, drew her weathered hand from her pocket and flung a fistful of fire dust into the eager flames.

Suddenly, from the center of a blinding flash, burst a broad shouldered eagle. The majestic bird swooped down and landed directly in front of Grandmother Earth Fire, then spoke to her in a strange tongue that evoked memories of an age, long vanished from consciousness. The voice of the bronze bird lulled the gathering into a dream-like state.

He then addressed the entire Council, "I am known to your Clan as Eagle Spirit. I am the shaman who prophesied the child, Hunete's, coming forth to claim the legacy of the Noble Janqua Clan. I heard your prayer and have come to serve the Council so the prophesy can be fulfilled."

The elders gasped. According to the legend, Eagle Spirit had lived in human form many generations ago. He was reputed to be an extraordinary healer and the most powerful leader the Clan had ever known.

Grandmother Earth Fire turned to Eagle Spirit and spoke, "We are honored and deeply grateful that you have returned to us now to help us fulfill the divine plan of our people. We need to devise a challenging initiation rite for the girl. We require your wisdom and healing magic."

With this welcome, Eagle Spirit and the Council eagerly engaged in a discussion that lasted until dawn. They agreed upon a plan that would begin immediately and come to completion at the ensuing full moon. On that day, the twelfth day, of the twelfth month, of the twelfth cycle of Ordinon, Hunete would turn twelve. When these celestial events fell into alignment, she would begin her initiation... a Vision Quest into the desert.

That morning Hunete's Grandfather presented the Council's decision to his granddaughter. At first, Hunete felt frightened. The memory of her father's disappearance still haunted her.

She didn't know what to expect, but she wasn't going to let anyone, including her Grandfather, notice that she was scared or confused. So she presented a smiling face to her guardian and said with as much enthusiasm as she could muster, "Great! I... I'm ready for anything. When do we start?"

Grandfather heard the slight tremble in Hunete's voice. He sighed a deep sigh and took her hands gently into his. A tear traveled slowly down the crevices in his weathered old cheek. His thoughts turned toward his son, lost to him forever, in the vast desert wasteland. Now the old man saw a spark of his son in the deep pool of his granddaughter's soft brown eyes. He spoke gravely, "This is a very serious decision for you. The Vision Quest will be dangerous. You *can* say no to this initiation and we will still love you. None of us will think any less of you."

Hunete was touched by her Grandfather's concern. For one brief moment, his softness melted the jagged edges of her heart. She longed for him to cradle her in his protective arms, to make her safe, as if held in the loving embrace of a proud father. Instead, she wiped the tear from her Grandfather's eye and declared, "I'll have none of that! I'm ready for anything. Nothing will stop me from winning that Vision Quest!"

"Dear one," the old man replied, "the Vision Quest is not a game to be won." Unfortunately, his words fell on deaf ears. So he looked to the heavens and spoke a silent prayer, releasing his own fear into the light and entrusting Hunete to the wisdom of Eagle Spirit.

Then Grandfather continued his instructions, "Hunete, you must attend the Great Fire of the Council of Elders for the next eleven nights to complete your training. Before the dawn of the twelfth day you will travel into the desert alone and complete the task the Council has devised for you."

Hunete gestured to her Grandfather that she understood, then quickly turned away. She stopped abruptly, looked back at her beloved guardian, and gave him a brisk hug. She smiled and said, "See you later," then turned, once again, and walked out of sight.

That night Hunete's belly was filled with a strange mixture of awe, excitement and dread. It was an immense honor to be invited to the Great Council Fire. She was the only initiate. The girl secretly delighted in the knowledge that the other children would envy her. Hunete liked being different. Yet, at the same time, a part of the girl wished she could just be one of the other children, with no special gifts and no initiation to face.

All night around the Great Fire, that blazed with the fierceness of the desert sun, the elders told heroic tales of their own Vision Quests into the barren land, conquering the monsters that lurked there.

Grandfather, a skilled story-teller in his own right, planted himself right in front of Hunete. He had her sitting on the edge of her seat as he described the deadly demons of the desert. "HUBRIS," he howled, "with eyes as big and green as honeydew melons, can devour, with a single, mighty gulp, any person who shows the least sign of self-doubt or insecurity."

"OBDURATUS," the old man roared, "is a ferocious beast with hairy arms, so strong they can tear giant redwoods out of the ground by their roots. He will easily overpower anyone who shows the slightest indication of a weakness of will."

Then the old man whispered, "The most terrifying devil of all is GEVAAR. He's a slimy creature who can smell human imperfection a hundred miles away."

Hunete gasped. Then Grandfather wailed above the murmurs of his spell-bound audience, "This clever beast will track you down no matter how hard you try to hide. Then he'll trap you in his snare. Frozen in his icy glare, he'll force you to admit defeat, then strangle you until the last ounce of breath drains from your lungs!"

Hunete was mesmerized by the details of these beasts, brimming with excitement about the possibility of confronting them with her own fierce strength and physical prowess. However, she didn't pay much attention to the rest of her grandfather's story.

"The only way," the old man continued, "to conquer these hideous monsters is to pray for help from the One Who is All Wise. Pray for humility, love, and the willingness to surrender your will to the greater will. In this way, you will receive the strength and wisdom you need to overcome your enemies."

As dawn of the twelfth day approached, after hearing story upon story upon story, Hunete insisted she was ready for her adventure in the desert. The Council of Elders granted her permission to begin the Vision Quest.

Grandfather approached his cherished grandchild, took her hands and spoke with deliberate care, "Hunete, you are to travel into the desert for twelve days and nights, seek out HUBRIS, OBDURATUS, and GEVAAR and vanquish them. You are not permitted to return to the village until you complete your ordeal or the twelve days have past."

He presented Hunete with a modest pouch of food, a water skin, and a small knife. These were the only provisions allowed. Suddenly, the bottom fell out of the girl's stomach. But, instead of seeking comfort and support from her Grandfather or the Council, Hunete once again hid behind her mask of invulnerability, turned and walked, without hesitation, away from the Great Fire toward the rising sun.

Hunete made her way down the footpath through the village, beyond the small creek that marked the boundary of the village, then traveled slowly but steadily past a stand of chaparral, into the open desert. The determined girl headed straight for Bat Mountain. She had heard of the magical properties of the caves carved out of the side of that towering peak by the wind and rain. Hunete hoped to find safe shelter there.

If I don't meet any of those monsters by the time I reach the base of the mountain, she thought, *I'll climb to the top. I'll be able to see for miles in every direction. No beast can hide from me there. Then I'll launch a surprise attack.*

By the end of the third day Hunete had reached the base of Bat Mountain. Along the way she had survived the harsh wilderness, foraging for edible plants, seeds, and tiny desert flowers. The clever girl conserved her precious water by using her small knife to cut sections from succulent cacti and sucking on the moist meat of the plants.

Only when absolutely necessary, Hunete hunted small rodents and snakes for food. As was the tradition of her Clan, she respected the plant and animal kingdoms, taking only what she needed and honoring everything she took.

That night, Hunete slept at the base of the mountain, careful not to build a fire just in case HUBRIS,

OBDURATUS, and GEVAAR were close by. After three long days in the hot sun, Hunete collapsed to the ground, but had difficulty falling asleep. As Hunete gave over to her need for rest, agonizing waves of self-doubt washed over the exhausted girl.

There was no one there to compete against, so she didn't have a way to win or judge herself to be better than anyone else. There was no one there to tell her how wonderful or brilliant or strong or clever she was. Alone, with only herself for company, she began to realize she wasn't in charge, there, in the vastness of the open wilderness. As clever as she was, Hunete couldn't manipulate herself out of her ordeal. *There's no way out of this,* she thought, *but to go through with it.*

Suddenly, danger flashed its warning light in the girl's mind. She remembered her Grandfather's warning that the desert beasts targeted human frailty. Anxious not to be ambushed, Hunete quickly suppressed her emotions and shut her eyes tightly. She repeated to herself over and over again, "I am stronger than my imperfections. I can beat those monsters any day," until she finally fell asleep.

The next morning, Hunete scaled the peak of Bat Mountain and carefully scanned the landscape. She saw no monsters... no desert beasts. In fact, she didn't see much of anything except miles and miles of sun parched wilderness. The girl seated herself on an outcropping of rock and waited.

Every few minutes she stood up sharply and stared out over the enormous expanse, hoping to catch a glimpse of HUBRIS, OBDURATUS, or GEVAAR. They were nowhere to be found. Day after day after day passed in this way.

Her impatience turned into frustration, her frustration into boredom, and her boredom into a gnawing hunger. More than anything, Hunete wanted to go home, to the warmth of the cooking fire and the sweet smell of vegetable stew bubbling in her grandmother's cast iron kettle. She particularly missed the other children, suddenly thinking of them as friends, instead of weaklings to be bullied. But in her mind, Hunete couldn't return, no matter how homesick, until she completed her mission.

Finally, by the end of the twelfth day in the desert, with no sign of the monsters and no more food or water, Hunete slipped into despair. The sun blazed hot on the back of her neck, her mouth was blistered and dry. The girl looked up and shouted toward the horizon, to anyone who might hear, to no one she could see, "I've failed. I am a disgrace to my family and the entire Clan. It's better to jump off this mountain and end my shame now, than go back home in defeat."

Hunete took three steps toward the edge of the overlook. As she placed her right foot over the ledge, ready to leap, some loose rocks shifted and the girl stumbled backward to safety. In the same moment, the girl also stumbled over some loose thoughts in her mind. Hunete remembered the prayer her grandfather had taught her.

She retreated from the ledge, turned to the north, raised her hands, palm up, to the sky and asked the Great Spirit to bless her. "I pray for humility. I wish to surrender to the greater will. I open my heart to love."

In the next moment, Hunete spotted a small shadow hovering above her in the pale blue sky. As the shadow drew close, Hunete could make out the elegant shape and fierce eyes of a golden eagle. The majestic bird of prey came to rest right next to the girl.

Hunete was startled by the strange tongue in which the eagle spoke. The sounds both frightened and comforted her. Much to her surprise, the girl understood every word. "I am Eagle Spirit. I am an emissary from the north. I bring you hope from the One Who is All Wise. How may I help?"

Hunete wept, "You're the answer to my prayers." Between sobs she managed to recount her story to the emissary from the spirit world. "I've been waiting and waiting for HUBRIS, OBDURATUS and GEVAAR to come out of hiding so I can kill them. That's why the elders sent me on this Vision Quest. But the monsters are nowhere. I've failed my test. I've lost... and worse, I'm all alone."

Eagle Spirit smiled, looked gently into the girl's eyes and said, "My dear child, there are no beasts. The only monsters in this desert are the dragons that live inside of you." Hunete looked quizzically at Eagle Spirit.

"You see, my dear, HUBRIS is your own pride that makes you want to win at all costs and be better than your friends. OBDURATUS is your willfulness that craves control and desperately needs to be right even when it serves no positive purpose. Last, but not least, is GEVAAR. GEVAAR is fear, your inner tyrant that rules with a perfectionistic iron fist."

The bronze bird continued, "When you're afraid of your own limitations, you keep them secret, trying to avoid the humiliation of what you imagine to be some terrible failure. However, it is the avoidance of mistakes, not that you make mistakes, that creates failure. So instead of feeling the momentary embarrassment of being imperfect, of being human, you stop trying. The only failure in life is not giving your best to it, even when giving your best means not being the best. Giving your best isn't about winning or not making mistakes, it's about trying."

"Pride, self-will and fear may have protected you from this embarrassment at one time, but they no longer serve you. They are now obstacles, barriers that keep you separate from others and stop you from bringing the light that is you out into the world. Hunete, these are the monsters the elders told you to confront and conquer here in the desert."

Hunete's mouth dropped open. She sensed the truth in the eagle's words, yet felt painfully exposed. "Oh, Eagle Spirit, I'm so ashamed I didn't figure this out myself. I guess I failed after all."

The bronze bird replied, "Child, there's your pride again. It serves you no purpose. It took real courage for you to journey into the desert alone and face yourself. This is the greatest success of all."

Hunete smiled, then laughed for the first time in days. "What a relief," she cried. "Thank you for your help. I'd like to go home now. I miss my family and my friends."

Eagle Spirit returned her grin and said, "Of course, my child, but first you must complete your rite of ascension. Are you truly willing to welcome humility, surrender and love into your heart? Say yes, and I will help you fulfill the prophesy of the Noble Janqua Clan."

Hunete was eager to hear more about the prophesy and complete her mission, "Yes, I say yes. I'll do anything. Just show me the way."

They stayed several more days at the top of Bat Mountain while the bronze eagle recounted the legend of the prophesy. He taught the girl to look inside herself for the truth and accept her imperfections. No longer driven by the powerful demons that ran her life from the shadows of her mind, Hunete began to feel, for the first time in her life, a deep sense of belonging.

As student and teacher said goodbye, Eagle Spirit reminded Hunete, "I am here for you always. Just say your prayer." Hunete embraced her guide, then he flew off toward the setting sun.

As she scrambled down the mountain Hunete realized she hadn't slept nor eaten, nor drank for days. Suddenly the weakened girl was surrounded by a pale peach light, the color of the sky just before dawn. Hunete knew then that she would be fine. Her longing for community drew her vulnerable body step by step, moment by moment toward her village, toward home.

Not only did Hunete return safely, but it took her less than half the time it took her to travel to Bat Mountain. She presented herself before the Council of Elders at the Great Fire.

Grandfather ran up to his beloved granddaughter, and with tears streaming down his face, drew her into his broad chest with his loving old arms. This time he noticed there were tears steaming down her face as well. "We had given up hope. We thought you were dead. But you're home, my precious one, you're home!"

The old man noticed the aura of light surrounding his grandchild and understood immediately that Hunete had conquered the desert dragons. Suddenly his booming voice could be heard above the crowd that had gathered, "Hunete, child of my child, seeker of truth and wisdom, you have successfully completed your Vision Quest. You are now ready to take your rightful place as the light bearer of our kin. You have returned to fulfill the divine purpose of the Noble Janqua Clan, the first tribe of the

Rainbow Warrior People... to bring our teachings into the world and usher in the Eternal Reign of Peace on this glorious planet."

With this proclamation, Grandfather led Hunete into the center of the sacred circle and painted her face with brilliant streaks of color. He then took her hands and in front of the others, with great pride and joy, gifted her the name, "Rainbow Warrior Woman".

The entire village clapped and cheered for their brave young warrior of peace. The elders proclaimed a day of celebration with dancing, singing and feasting. As the birch bark drums beat out ancient rhythms and the children chased each other around the Great Fire, the cry of an eagle rang out true and clear. Hunete looked up to the heavens and quietly, in her heart, thanked Eagle Spirit for his loving guidance, then joined in the fun.

JENNIFER'S MYSTERIOUS DISEASE

ong ago, in the duchy of Blitherbottom, in the county of Hystrionia, on the tiny island country of Duality, lived a little girl named Jennifer. Jennifer dwelled in a beautiful, two hundred room mansion on a magnificent estate with her parents, the Duke and Duchess of Blitherbottom. She was an only child, so the Duke and Duchess pampered her, lavishing her with exquisite clothes and extraordinary toys. "Nothing but the best for my little girl," the Duchess would always say.

Jennifer, however, was not really interested in such things. She enjoyed playing kickball with the servants' children and wandering through the woods with her loveable and luscious brown Labrador retriever, named Chocolate Cherry Pie.

Jennifer frequently let Cherry Pie chase her down to Blue Haven Pond. The energetic child loved to throw sticks into the water for her furry brown companion to fetch. Sometimes, in her excitement, Jennifer would vault into the water and retrieve the sticks herself.

When the girl arrived home wet and muddy, accompanied by her very doggy smelling dog, her mother would bustle about with her nose in the air, banishing Cherry Pie to the stable, to be bathed by the grooms in sickly sweet perfumes. Jennifer suffered the same fate in the upstairs tub at the hands of her nanny.

Neither of them liked that very much. But even worse was the scolding Jennifer always received from her mother. The Duchess would wring her hands, as she paced back and forth in front of the bathtub, "Oh, my dear, sweet Jennifer, it is a trifle bit annoying when you come home soaking wet and caked with mud. These new clothes I had made for you are ruined. You know better than that. It's just not like a little lady to jump into ponds and fetch sticks."

Then the Duchess would wring her hands some more, pleading with her vigorous child, "And besides, my dearest, I do worry so that you'll catch your death of cold, running hither and thither in wet hair and damp clothes. I just wish you would act more like me, a noble woman of breeding."

By the end of her speech, the Duchess invariably forgave Jennifer, smothered her with hugs and kisses, and insisted on a promise from her high-spirited daughter. "Now, promise your Mum that you'll never jump in that dreadful pond again."

With her fingers crossed behind her back, Jennifer would say in her sweetest voice, "Yes, Mother Dear, I promise."

Then, the doting mother tucked her daughter into bed under a wool blanket, with a steaming hot cup of tea. Jennifer liked this part of their ritual the least. It could be the middle of a sweltering summer's day and there she would lay, curled up in her bed, bored and sweaty, just to appease her overly-protective mother.

The Duchess panicked if Jennifer walked in the door with nothing more than a scraped knee. The delirious Duchess immediately summoned a team of physicians and healers, insisting in a loud voice, "You must fix this problem right now! I don't want my precious little girl to suffer a moment's pain."

Whenever Jennifer fell into a bit of a blue mood, the grand dame of Blitherbottom bade every clown and jester, every musician and minstrel in the county to appear before the child to cheer her up.

Of course, Jennifer refused to take part in this nonsense. She wasn't concerned if she scraped a knee or felt a bit down in the dumps. She knew the scratch would heal and her mood would change. And as long as she remembered who she was inside, she believed that everything would work out just fine.

Unfortunately, Jennifer's mother didn't share this same faith in life. The doting mother's immediate response to the slightest injury was to, "fix the problem" and "make the pain go away." Even though the Duchess was truly concerned for her daughter, it was really her own discomfort that was intolerable to her.

Jennifer hated her mother's perspective on life, but loved her dearly. The little girl was determined not to add to her mother's anxiety, so she did whatever she thought would make her mother happy.

However, Jennifer's nature was not easily bridled. So after the dust settled from each crisis, she'd sneak out of the mansion, run down to the pond with her dog and once again, leap into the wet, slimy ooze.

One late afternoon toward the end of a most brilliant and dazzling summer, Jennifer lingered in the lagoon until dusk, having lost track of the time. When the girl realized how late it was, she hastily gathered up her clothes and her doggy smelling dog, bolted down the path in the woods, through the meadow, up the lawn and directly upstairs to her bedroom. By that time, Jennifer had a bit of a sniffle and a touch of an ache in her bones. She thought, *oh no, now I've done it. I've caught a cold. Mum will have a real snit this time.*

Just as she finished her thought, Jennifer's mother descended upon her daughter. After several minutes of smothering hugs and numerous exclamations, "Oh, I thought you were dead! Oh, I am so glad you're alive! Oh, look at your clothes!" the Duchess tucked Jennifer, safely and snugly, into bed with a hot cup of tea and some toast. This time the girl eagerly curled up underneath her warm wool blanket and soon fell fast asleep.

When she awoke, Jennifer discovered both her parents and her poor nanny positioned carefully around her bed, watching with great interest. The girl sneezed and then coughed. Instantaneously, the three alarmed nursemaids flew out of their seats and launched into frenzied fussing.

Before Jennifer could protest, her mother ordered Nanny to summon all the physicians and the healers in the county of Hystrionia. "Nanny, wait!" Jennifer insisted. "Mother, I just caught a bit of a cold. There's really nothing to worry about. I'm fine, really. Please don't call the doctors."

But the doting Duchess ignored her daughter's protests. She gestured to Nanny, then paced back and forth in front of the bed, wringing her hands anxiously, while the nursemaid ran out the door.

When the physicians and healers arrived, they spent hours poking and prodding the hapless little girl. By the time they finished examining her, her body was covered with black and blue marks. Jennifer felt much worse than before.

The Duchess anxiously awaited the physicians' assessment. She paced back and forth, mumbling under her breath, "Oh my God, what's wrong with my beloved child? What's wrong, what's wrong, what's wrong?" The Duchess was in the throws of a full blown panic attack by the time the physicians reported their findings.

"My Lady," several spoke at once, "your dear little girl has contracted a mild cold. She'll recover with a few days of rest."

The medical practitioners were surprised to find that instead of calming her down, their news only served to increase the Duchess's distress. She screamed, "You bumbling idiots! Can't you see there's something terribly wrong with my daughter! You have to fix her! You have to make her better! NOW!"

The Duchess pointed to the girl and yelled, "Look! She's sniffling and sneezing and now she has bruises all over her body! She's getting worse. You have to find out what's wrong with her!"

The doctors conferred with each other in whispers, scratching their heads, glancing quizzically at Jennifer, then at the Duchess, then back toward the little girl. Finally, the chief physician promised to examine Jennifer again. The commotion had given the little girl a headache. The physicians and healers poked and prodded some more, making comments about her condition, "Look," one would say, "her complexion is all wrong." Then another would opine, "Looks like a serious defect in her immune system."

Each time one of the healers expressed a judgement or opinion about her body, another sharp pain or dull aching knot would arise. Jennifer knew deep inside there was nothing wrong with her, so their judgements just made her feel worse.

By the time the physicians and healers finished their second evaluation, they were convinced the girl was, indeed, terribly ill. They noticed the unusual bruises and were startled to learn that Jennifer was now complaining about a headache, sharp pains and dull aching knots.

The baffled medical practitioners consulated with one another again. Then the chief physician pulled the apprehensive mother aside, cupped his hand over her ear and whispered, "My Lady, I regret to inform you that your daughter has a strange and mysterious disease that we've never encountered before. We'll do everything we can for her, but we don't know if she'll recover."

The Duchess stopped wringing her hands, sat down calmly next the bed and sighed, "I knew there was something terribly wrong with my daughter. I'll take care of her."

The chief physician was incredulous. He whispered a bit louder, but not loud enough for Jennifer to hear, "My Lady, did you hear what I said? Your daughter is very sick."

"Yes, I heard you."

"Duchess, your daughter may spend the rest of her life in bed."

"I understand." The Duchess sighed dreamily, her thoughts somewhere else. *At least I'll know where she is. At least I'll know she's safe. I'll sit right here by her side and take care of my precious little girl forever.*

The grand dame of Blitherbottom was secretly relieved that she now controlled her child's future... that she could keep Jennifer safe for the rest of her life. *I know what's best for My Precious,* she thought. *I'll take away her pain and make my little girl happy. Then I'll never be anxious again.* Of course, the Duchess didn't stop to think how Jennifer might feel about all of this.

The chief physician didn't understand why this dreadful news seemed to calm the Duchess. However, he decided if he wanted to keep his job, he'd better keep quiet and do whatever she demanded.

For the next few days, the physicians and healers took turns around the clock poking and prodding the little girl, making judgements and offering opinions about her condition, and saturating her with a myriad of medicines, drugs, and elixirs. These treatments just made her worse.

By the end of the fourth day, Jennifer couldn't keep anything in her stomach and couldn't sit up in bed. Worst of all, she began to think of herself as an invalid. She thought, *I'm worthless. I can't do any of the things I used to do. I feel really bad inside.*

By the end of the fifth day, the little girl felt hopeless. She floated in and out of consciousness, moaning, "I can't remember who I am. I can't remember."

Then Cherry Pie, sensing Jennifer's distress, put her big, square jaw on top of the bed and gently licked her human's tiny hand with her floppy pink tongue. In one brief moment of remembering, fury welled up from the depths of the weakened girl's heart. "Go away and leave me alone," she screamed through her coughs. "You're all treating me like a thing that's broken and needs to be fixed, not like a whole person. Just leave me alone! I want to die!"

The exhausted child wept. Her mother rushed to her bedside, fussing and making cheerful suggestions about how to feel better. That only made Jennifer cry louder. The Duke dragged his wife away from the bed and, being careful not to offend her, calmly suggested, "Why don't we leave the child alone for a bit and let her rest." As the entourage withdrew, Jennifer sighed a deep sigh of relief, falling quickly asleep.

In the quiet stillness of the night, Jennifer woke to the sound of rustling. Cherry Pie stood at attention, her floppy-jowled snout resting on the window sill, gazing intently at the full moon.

Suddenly, a shaft of moonlight broke through the window. Jennifer sat up quickly, her eyes bugging out, as a tiny sparkle of light traveled the length of the moonbeam, through the window, touching down lightly on the throw rug at the base of the bed.

The sparkle expanded into a giant sphere of shimmering white light, enveloping Jennifer and Cherry Pie. Then a figure emerged from the sphere. She wore a flowing white cloak that shimmered in the moonlight, as if every inch of it was covered with diamonds.

Jennifer's mouth dropped open as this dazzling being floated gently across the room toward her bed. The girl was a bit confused. *Maybe it's the drugs,* she thought.

Then her body gave over to the light and the little girl felt calm for the first time in days. Jennifer stumbled on her words, "Wh... who are you?"

The light being gazed into Jennifer's eyes and spoke in a divinely harmonious voice, "I am Gabriela, your spirit guide."

"My what?"

Gabriela smiled sweetly, then lightened her tone, "I'm an angel. You know, like your fairy godmother... or something."

Jennifer was embarrassed. She giggled nervously, then challenged the being. "You're no angel...you don't have any wings."

Gabriela laughed, then without saying a word spun around quickly and removed her cape. Two enormous wings popped out of her back, nearly filling the entire bedroom.

The glorious being giggled, turned around and said, "It's a lot easier to travel on moonbeams when you pack the old wings underneath the cape. They're rather large, you see, and sometimes a bit dangerous."

Cherry Pie had ducked under the bed to avoid getting bopped on the head. She tentatively poked her nose out from the pink, ruffled bed-skirt, to sniff the stranger, whom she knew right away was not human.

Jennifer laughed. It was the first time she'd laughed for days. It felt good. "So, if you're my angel, why are you here now?"

Gabriela explained, "I sensed your despair and knew you'd forgotten who you are. I'm here to remind you. That's what angels do."

Jennifer felt at ease with her new friend and quickly recounted the story of her growing illness, "Everyone's treating me like some broken thing. That feels more awful than being sick in the first place. The worst thing of all is that I *have* forgotten who I really am, and no matter how hard I try, I just can't seem to remember."

Gabriela listened carefully. Then she placed her hand tenderly on Jennifer's forehead, scanned her energy system, and touched into the greater wisdom of the girl's soul. She sat back on her wings, put her hand to her chin, pausing to integrate the messages she'd received.

The guardian angel looked lovingly at the girl and said, "Now that I've done my examination, here's my assessment. You're fine. There's nothing *wrong* with you. You still have a bit of a cold, that's all. You're perfectly whole. Frankly, I don't see what all the fuss is about. Even if you'd had a terrible disease and died, you'd still be fine. You're still the free-spirited, curious child you've always been."

Jennifer sighed a massive sigh of relief, "I thought so. I just couldn't remember. But I don't understand why everyone else seems to think I'm so sick."

"Well," sighed Gabriela. "You see, Jennifer, most people in Duality look at every experience as either good or bad. They always focus on what's wrong or right and mostly only notice what's wrong. Instead of seeing you as a whole person with a cold, your family and the doctors saw you as broken person who needed to be fixed. The more they focused on what they thought was wrong, the sicker you became, until you forgot your wholeness. Eventually you, too, believed you were broken and that's why you wanted to die."

Jennifer's eyes brightened. "So I'm not broken? I'm still me?"

"Yes, my dear." The angel scooped up the girl in her arms and rocked her. Jennifer wept quietly.

The little girl's heart broke free from its cage of despair. For the first time in days, Jennifer felt alive.

Jennifer stared into the shimmering angel's eyes and said, "But how do I make them see that I don't need to be fixed?"

"For three days and three nights you must refuse to be examined or evaluated. You mustn't take drugs or elixirs or receive treatment of any kind. At the end of that time, you'll remember everything."

"But Gabriela," the girl protested, "My mother won't like that idea at all. Besides, it sounds kind of scary."

"My dear Jennifer," the angel replied, "If you want to reclaim your spirit, you must put aside your mother's beliefs about life and find your own way. I know it's a scary path, but I'll walk with you back into your wholeness."

"You'll stay with me the whole time?" the little girl squeaked.

The angel took Jennifer's hand, then crossed her own heart, and with firm resolve in her voice said, "I promise."

The little girl squeezed her angel's hand, then summoned her parents. Gabriela grew small, disguising herself as a flame in the oil lamp on Jennifer's bedside table.

"You want to do what!" the Duchess exclaimed, after Jennifer explained she didn't want anyone in her chamber for three days and would refuse all medicine. The Duchess's distress increased tenfold every minute. She started to wring her hands and pace back and forth, wearing a path in the rug at the foot of the bed.

Then she turned to the Duke, her arms waving excitedly, "Harold, did you hear what she said? I think she's delirious! Quick, call the chief physician."

Jennifer hesitated, then saw the flame in the oil lamp burn brighter and cried, "Mother! Don't you dare call that doctor. I know what I want. I know what's best for me."

The Duchess's fear turned quickly to force, "Jennifer, you must let the physicians minister to you or I'll tie you to the bed myself and make you take your medicine!"

Jennifer was aghast. "If you try anything like that, I'll refuse to eat. That's right, I'll starve myself to death."

Then the girl softened a bit. "Mother, I don't want to be an invalid forever. The only way for me to feel better is to remember that I'm whole. But I can't do that if everyone keeps telling me I'm broken. I'm not broken, Mother. I don't need to be fixed."

Jennifer noticed the deep lines of doubt on the Duchess's face. "I'm safe... besides I won't be entirely alone."

The grand dame dubiously eyed the chocolate brown dog lying patiently by the side of her daughter's bed. Jennifer smiled. "Really, I'm safe, I promise."

The bewildered Duchess realized that her daughter's mind was made up. It seemed that their only option was to stand watch outside the door, just in case Jennifer cried for help.

The Duke, then the grand dame of Blitherbottom, kissed Jennifer on her forehead and exited the room. They took turns with their ears to the door, hoping to hear the slightest noise, some sign that Jennifer needed them.

For the next three days Gabriela sat next to the bed, gripped the girl's hands, wiped her brow with a cool, damp cloth and fed her hot tea and toast. The magnificent winged being cradled Jennifer in her arms and whispered, "Dear little one, I'm so glad you are you. You're perfectly whole and fill up the world with light. I'm so glad you're alive."

Not once in three days did Gabriela judge the little girl, try to fix her, compel her to feel better, or heal her. After three days of headaches and nausea, Jennifer recovered. She remembered her wholeness.

Gabriela hid in the oil lamp, again, as Jennifer invited her parents to come back in the room. The Duke and Duchess looked as if they hadn't slept or eaten for three days. When the Duchess saw her smiling daughter, sitting upright in bed, eating her toast, the grand dame burst into tears, dashed to the bed and smothered her little girl in kisses. This time Jennifer didn't mind. The

Duke stood by, with a broad grin on his face and his arms folded across his puffed-up chest.

Jennifer held out her hands to her parents and with an impish glint in her eye announced, "Look Mother, look Father, I've healed myself."

Suddenly, the Duchess stiffened her back, stormed out of the bedroom, waving her arms wildly. She glared at the physicians and healers who'd been milling about in the hallway and shouted, "Get out! My brilliant daughter has healed herself. You're all fired. Get out!" Then they all packed their little black bags and indignantly marched out of the mansion.

When the Duchess returned to Jennifer's bedside, she seized the girl's hands and cried, "My one and only child. I love you dearly. I promise I'll never try to fix you again or force you to be something you're not."

Jennifer wrapped her arms around the Duchess and laughed, "I'm so glad to hear you say that." Jennifer squeezed her mother tightly, then released her. "I need a little more rest. We can talk more later."

Jennifer asked her parents to leave. The Duke and Duchess looked perplexed, but were eager to oblige their brilliant daughter who had miraculously healed herself of a strange and mysterious disease.

As the Duke and Duchess retreated, Gabriela reappeared, in her fullness, by Jennifer's bedside. She leaned over and offered the youngster a glorious angel hug. Jennifer kissed the winged being on the cheek and thanked her, "You never tried to make me better."

Gabriela replied, "My dear, how could I have possibly made you better than you already are. My divine child, you are perfectly whole and always have been."

With that, the seraph grew small again, into a tiny sparkle of light and flew out the window. This time she caught a ride on a passing rainbow. As she soared out of sight, the little girl heard that sweet angel voice, "I'll always come whenever you call. Remember your wholeness."

Jennifer sighed, then turned to her chocolate colored companion, gave her a big bear hug and giggled, "Looks like a good day for jumping in ponds and fetching sticks... What do you say!" In the next instant, Cherry Pie pounced on the bed and licked Jennifer's face with her enormous pink tongue. The little girl laughed a huge belly laugh and said, "I guess that means yes!"

THE WATERBUG

$\mathcal{J}$ amie blasted out of bed as her alarm clock sounded from a bookshelf on the opposite side of the room. It was the only way she could force herself out of a deep sleep at five thirty in the morning. Even though it was summer vacation, Jamie knew her mother would not wake up until noon and since she was the oldest, it was her responsibility to make sure the day proceeded as scheduled.

Jamie grabbed her robe. As her feet touched the floor, Rosie, the girl's sable and white Shetland sheepdog, scooted under the bed to avoid being trampled by her human, seizing the moment to conceal herself until the frenzy of this morning ritual subsided.

Rosie was a beautiful, but sometimes officious creature. Her sole purpose in life was to keep her human out of harm's way by herding the youngster around the yard. Rosie knew instinctively that Jamie needed love. So that's what she did and she did it quite well.

Jamie lived in a comfortable split-level in the suburbs with her mother, father, and two brothers. Her father was a salesman, often away on business trips. The girl's mother hardly ever got out of bed. So, at the ripe old age of ten, Jamie became mother and father, chief cook and bottle washer to her two younger brothers.

By seven each morning, Jamie had put down fresh food and water for Rosie, cleaned the bathroom, put in a load of laundry, fed the boys microwave pancakes with sausage, and dispatched them to day camp with the next door neighbor. Then she would tip toe into her mother's room, "quiet as a mouse," to make sure she was still breathing and had easy access to her "medicine" on the night stand adjacent to her bed.

Then and only then, was Jamie free to relax. She loved to laze around the swimming pool in the back yard and watch the world, noticing all the creatures that slithered and soared and crept and crawled within view. That is... until her mother called for her.

Jamie's mom had, what her father called, a "problem with her nerves." Jamie didn't really understand why her mother squandered her time watching soap operas, sobbing into her pillow, and sipping sherry out of a flask labeled nerve tonic. Her mom always seemed so sad. This broke Jamie's heart. She loved her mother very much.

So Jamie tended to her mother, trying to comfort her. The girl raced to her bedside whenever the fragile woman called. She soothed her mother's brow, fluffed her pillows, dispensed the green and white capsules the doctors prescribed, and delivered coffee and plain toast, which was all her mother was able to eat at times. The youngster even walked the mile and a half to the liquor store each afternoon, to collect the bottle of sherry her mother ordered from the owner, a friend of the family.

Jamie hated this chore, but whenever she hesitated, her mother screamed uncontrollably, "You're such an ungrateful child! That sherry is my 'medicine.' It's my only real comfort in life."

Jamie's response was always the same, "I'm sorry, Mom. Please, please don't be upset. I'll go see Mr. Brown right away and get your medicine."

Jamie was stymied as to how to manage her mother's uncontrollable mood swings. Each day, as she quickened her pace to the liquor store, the girl gave herself a negative pep talk, "That was stupid, J. You made her mad again. Just do what she says and be super, extra nice."

Jamie's father was not much help. He was away from home most of the time and when he returned, he'd provoke arguments with his wife. "You're good-for-nothing," he'd scream, dragging her by her feet off the bed. "Why don't you get out of that tomb and act like a real wife and mother!"

In the next instant, he'd seize her flask. In a desperate attempt to rescue her "medicine" from his clutches, the intoxicated woman would grasp at her husband's hands, stumbling after him into the bathroom. "Gimme dat," she'd slur. "Dat's my medcine." Then she'd collapse to her knees, engulfed in a pool of tears, as he'd pour the toxic liquid into the toilet and flush.

Jamie had witnessed this scene countless times. It tore her apart. Jamie couldn't tolerate her feelings of helplessness when she saw someone in pain.

She was constantly bringing home lost puppies and kittens, which her father was constantly bringing right back to the local animal shelter. Jamie was always disappointed, but kept quiet. She didn't want to cause a fuss.

One of the girl's favorite pastimes was lying around by the side of the swimming pool, rescuing drowning bugs. When the sympathetic child spied a helpless insect, a bumble bee perhaps, spinning wildly out-of-control on the surface of the water, she'd grab the skimmer, scoop it up gently, then set it down on the cement walkway surrounding the pool. Then she'd monitor the bug until it dried its wings and flew away. Satisfied, after successfully completing a rescue mission, Jamie would give herself a positive pep talk, "There you go J., you've once again saved one of God's creatures. You done good!"

Jamie wished it could be that simple with her mother. In her child's mind, she envisioned herself with a giant skimmer, rushing to her helpless mother's bedside, scooping her right up out of her pool of misery. Of course, Jamie knew this was a daydream. In reality, she'd just have to muddle along, as best as she could.

One bright, sunny day after Jamie finished her chores and glanced in on her mother to make certain she was okay, the little grown-up girl summoned her faithful companion, Rosie, and retreated to her favorite site by the swimming pool. She exhausted several hours mindlessly scooping up tiny, helpless creatures, depositing them gently on the sidewalk, and watching them fly off into the brilliant blue sky.

Curiously, the youngster noticed that one of the bugs did not fly away. Instead, it thrashed about, desperately flip-flopping back and forth over the cement. Jamie knelt down to get a better look. *This bug,* she thought, *is not acting like any other bug I've ever saved.*

Suddenly, Jamie realized she had inadvertently scooped a waterbug out of the pool. "Oh my God!" she gasped. "He's drowning in the air!" She quickly snatched up the insect in a desperate attempt to return him to the water... but it was too late. The waterbug was already dead.

Jamie stood paralysed, gaping at the dead insect. She had inadvertently killed a living being in her zest to save it. A wave of guilt turned the girl's stomach inside out.

Sobbing uncontrollably she cried, "I've killed the poor bug... My God, what've I done!"

The sable and white Sheltie patiently watched this scene, then true to her nature, nuzzled up to her human, wagged her tail, and licked the tears away from Jamie's face. But the girl was inconsolable. Jamie hurled the skimmer and bolted through the yard to the footpath at the entrance of the woods near the border of the family's property, with Rosie following right at her heels.

Jamie sprinted for nearly a mile, until she found herself in an unfamiliar section of the woods. She stopped in her tracks, her thoughts racing in a futile attempt to stave off the fear that slowly crept up her spine. "I'm lost," she whispered to the trees. Jamie knelt down, scooped up her little dog and grasped Rosie tightly to her chest. Then Jamie buried her head into her pet's silky fir coat and wept until her tears ran dry.

Suddenly, the girl heard a trace of another's breath. Jamie jerked her head up, startled to discover a tall, slender figure of a woman standing over her. Rosie vaulted out of her human's arms, barking incessantly at the intruder with a force so fierce every muscle, from the top of her pointy snout to the tip of her silky tail, reverberated with her own voice. Jamie sprang to her feet.

The woman was young, perhaps no more than twenty. Her straight, jet black hair cascaded down her shoulders to the middle of her back. She wore a buckskin tunic tied at her waist with a beaded belt. The handsome figure knelt down, holding her hand out, palm up, to the barking body of fur. Rosie sniffed, then relaxed. Her ears flattened and her tail, then the entire back half of her body, began to wag.

With a calm, clear voice the young woman turned to Jamie and said, "You have a beautiful little dog. She is very sweet and very protective of you... that is good. My name is Little Bear. How are you called?"

Jamie stared, wide-eyed and mouth gaping, at this exotic woman. Jamie thought the stranger was like some character out of an old television show or perhaps a legend, lost and forgotten in time.

The girl's voice trembled as she stumbled over her words, "M..my name is Jamie... this is Rosie. Wh..who are you? What are you doing in these woods?"

"So many questions, my young friend," the enchanted stranger replied. "I will answer them all. But first let me guide you to shelter. The sky will soon shower us with rain and night descends quickly."

Jamie was dumbfounded. Just two minutes ago, it was the middle of a bright, sunny day. Now, when she looked into the sky she saw dark clouds gathering and the sun quietly setting beyond the western horizon.

Suddenly, Jamie turned toward where she thought her house was and cried out in a panic, "You don't understand. I've got to get home before dark. My mother needs me. She'll never manage by herself!"

"Be still, child." Little Bear gently took Jamie's hand. "Time has no meaning in this place. When you are ready to return home, I will lead you to the correct path and you will find yourself back where you began this journey, as if no time at all has passed."

Jamie addressed the tall woman, "I don't really believe you, but I guess I'll go with you because I don't know my way home... and it *is* getting dark." The girl became more assertive, "But I want you to know that I'll leave whenever I want, and if you try anything funny I'll sic my dog on you! She may be small, but she's got very sharp teeth!" Rosie heard the change in Jamie's voice and added a yap or two for good measure.

Little Bear smiled, gently honoring Jamie's boundary. "I have no doubt your trusted companion is a formidable foe, and you may certainly leave whenever you wish. I have no desire to detain you. My only hope is that you will visit with me a while. I am lonely and I have many stories to tell. You might even find a grain of truth in them, useful to you on your life's path."

As soon as the mysterious woman said she was lonely, the needle on Jamie's internal sympathy meter went off the scale. She eagerly followed the tall, dark woman back to her shelter.

The three of them walked at a steady pace, while Jamie considered the unusual woman's circumstance, *I bet she is lonely, living out here in the woods with no one to talk to.* But in the back of her mind lurked anxious thoughts about her mother.

Little Bear directed Jamie and the Sheltie to a lodge made from long birch poles, bowed to form a dome. The structure was covered with animal hides. It resembled a small igloo from the outside. Once inside, however, the quarters were spacious. The ceiling of the lodge was high enough to accommodate both Jamie and the tall stranger standing. Then, magically, each time Jamie came to the edge of a room, an archway appeared, leading to another chamber.

As Jamie adjusted to the dim light in the main room, she noticed simple, stick-figure drawings of animals on the walls, and multi-colored crystals, feathers and candles neatly arranged around a stone cooking pit. As the girl absorbed the beauty of her surroundings, she gently lapsed into a pleasant state of quiet attention that reminded her of that space between wakefulness and sleep, when the worries of the day slip away in the mist of forgetting. Jamie glanced at the far corner of the lodge where Rosie lay peacefully asleep on a bearskin rug.

Little Bear invited Jamie to settle down on a feather pillow on the earthen floor. She then handed the girl a cup of warm herb broth, whose sweet nourishment tickled the back of her throat and quieted the girl's rumbling belly.

The tall dark figure considered Jamie for a moment, then said, "If you please, I will tell you a story now, then we will talk."

Jamie nodded her head. Little Bear began. "Once upon a time, there was a young girl who took upon her shoulders the suffering of the whole world. This girl felt great compassion for others, but in her zeal to help, she neglected her own needs. And sometimes in trying so hard to be so good, she caused more harm than good; like the bright, sunny day she absent-mindedly killed a waterbug, thinking she was saving a bumble bee from the jaws of death."

Jamie's chin dropped to her chest, "Who are you? What is this place? How did you know about the waterbug?"

The mysterious woman replied, in a voice that seemed distant and dreamlike to the child, "My young friend, I am, indeed, a character from an ancient legend, long ago vanished from the hearts of everyday folk... but I was not lost. I live in this Dream Lodge and come to those who need a story, a trail-marker to point them back to their true path. So I came to you, this day, in your most desperate moment of forgetting."

Jamie felt the warm moistness of tears, sweetly bathing her soft, round cheeks. The vulnerable child cried, "Will you help me then? I want to know how I could've done such an awful thing, killing that waterbug. And why do I feel other people's pain so strongly?"

The mythical being spoke in a sweet, soothing tone, "Dear friend, your heart is wide open. This is good. Compassion is a beautiful gift when tempered with humility. It is presumptuous to think that it is your responsibility to take away someone else's pain. And such a burden to bear. It is a delicate matter to interfere with another soul's journey. You might rob them of their real healing.

"Hold others in the loving embrace of your compassion, but let them live their lives as they were meant to be lived. The waterbug died because you rescued him when he did not need to be rescued. When you bring your mother her 'medicine,' you rob her of the opportunity to face her own truth. Who's to say what another's path is?"

Jamie leapt to her feet and screamed, "No, it's not true! I can't just sit by and helplessly watch when she hurts so much."

"Sometimes," Little Bear replied, "the most compassionate act is to simply bear witness to another's pain, with love in your heart."

Jamie collapsed in a pool of tears. "I can't do it. I don't know how."

Little Bear reached over to the distraught girl and placed a hand lightly on her shoulder. "Stay with me for a time, young friend. I will tell you stories about the natural rhythms and cycles of life. You might discover, in their images and words, wisdom for your heart, that will open you to true compassion. Then you will know exactly how to be with your mother. When it is right, you will feel it in your bones."

Jamie looked into the eyes of the tall, dark woman who'd appeared before her in her hour of need, and noticed a strange tingling in her elbow. "You're right, Little Bear," she smiled, "I do feel it in my bones. I'll stay and hear your stories."

Jamie remained with Little Bear for the rest of the summer. As the days waned shorter, the maples, ash trees, birches and oaks of the magical woods turned brilliant shades of crimson, gold, orange and yellow, and a feisty north wind began frosting the edges of the ground every morning.

One day, Little Bear turned toward the north, tested the wind with her hand and spoke, "We must prepare for the Dreamtime."

The girl inquired, "What's that?"

"It is a period of introspection, a time of going inside to seek your soul's longing. It will last all winter. In the spring you will be ready to return home."

Jamie helped Little Bear prepare the Dream Lodge. Rosie, who'd lived happily in the woods with her human, free from the stress of hiding under the bed each morning, eagerly herded every furry creature she could find, expertly guiding them to their homes for the long, cold winter.

When the preparations were complete, Jamie, Rosie and Little Bear crawled into the Dream Lodge and sat huddled together near the cooking fire. Covered with heavy fur blankets, Jamie instantaneously lapsed into a dreamy inner state.

The girl walked carefully through a thick fog, then suddenly found herself standing at her mother's bedside. Jamie watched and waited.

Her mother sipped and sipped and sipped, until the last drop of liquid rolled out the flask onto her tongue. The intoxicated woman flung the metal container across the room and cried out to her daughter, who stood motionless in plain view, "Jamie, go see Mr. Brown and tell him I need more medicine. He'll know what to do."

Jamie did not budge. She took a deep breath.

"Why are you just standing there? I told you I *need* my medicine. Please, don't you understand? It's my only comfort."

The woman's pleading pulled at the young girl's heart. It required every ounce of energy and effort she could muster to refrain from rushing to her mother's side, grabbing the money from her purse and running out the door.

Instead, Jamie stayed focused on herself, gazed intently at her mother and said, "Mom, I love you dearly. In fact, I love so much, I'm never going to the liquor store for you again."

The intoxicated woman screamed, "You've betrayed me, you ungrateful child!" Then she curled up into a tight ball and sobbed into her pillow.

Jamie felt her mother's anguish. The girl's body trembled with a shock wave of helplessness, then her stomach turned inside out. But she didn't do anything. She waited and watched, opening to her own experience and holding her mother tenderly in her heart.

Jamie took another deep breath, then suddenly found herself, once again, in the Dream Lodge, curled up next to her faithful companion and her new friend. Little Bear awoke and opened the door to the lodge. The three of them crawled outside to meet a gorgeous spring day. The air was dry and cool, but the sun felt warm on their faces as they stretched and yawned and wiped the sleep from their eyes.

Little Bear turned to Jamie, placed her arm gently around the girl and said, "You have learned what you came here to learn. It is time for you to return home."

Jamie gathered up her little sable and white dog. The three companions headed back down the path to the point where they'd first met. Little Bear turned to her friend and said, "I will miss you. We must part now, but always remember the Dream Lodge. You can return here anytime you need guidance or support."

Before Jamie could respond, Little Bear disappeared into the woods. As she watched the dark figure trail off into the distance, the girl heard the faint rumbling growl of a bear.

The startled child rushed to where she thought the path to the Dream Lodge began, but that, too, had disappeared. Jamie walked a bit farther into the dense undergrowth. The only evidence of Little Bear's presence was several enormous paw prints, freshly laid in the soft, warm earth. Jamie smiled. A velvety giggle rippled up the back of her throat.

As Jamie walked out of the woods, Rosie right at her heels, she noticed the sun had moved much higher in the sky and the air was suddenly quite humid. In a flash, Jamie realized that she had, in fact, returned to that very moment in time last summer when she fled from the pool in a panic after killing the waterbug. She smiled again and thought, *just as Little Bear promised.*

With a new faith in the cycles of life and a heart open wide to the wisdom of real compassion, Jamie approached the back door and turned the knob. She was, indeed, ready to return home.

THE FLOWERING

In the earliest moments of spring, just as the last crust of white melted from the near corner of the old English Garden, the tiniest, most brilliant shoot of vibrant green propelled itself through the surface of the half-frozen earth. As the days waxed longer and the sun crept higher in the sky, striving with unwavering purpose toward its zenith, the Little Green Flowering Essence grew a tiny bud at the peak of her stem. This small flower, eagerly anticipating its full blossoming into life, longed for the unbounded light and warmth of the sun.

One morning, the old gardener gathered up his tools and painstakingly made his way from the neatly trimmed tool shed to the south side of the garden to initiate his yearly ritual of removing the half-rotten mulch from around the edges of the new shoots, in hopes of easing their struggle upward. As he entered the flowerbed, the old man carelessly stepped on top of the Little Green Flowering Essence. Because she was so small and he was so large and had very little eyesight left, he simply didn't notice the tiny green shoot in his haste to complete his task.

The Little Green Flowering Essence lay crushed on her side, hugging the still slightly hard earth, squashed by the very being whose job it was to nurture, support, and encourage her to grow. The tiny shoot lay motionless, numb from the shock of this sudden turn of life, the apparent betrayal of her trusted caretaker.

She thought, *this garden certainly isn't very safe, is it? And he... well, he's just an old fool.* The crumpled flower choked back her tears, then forced into some hidden corner of her awareness the torrent of emotions that were struggling to find expression within her. In that moment, the Little Green Flowering Essence decided she would never trust anyone. *I guess I'll just have to grow up myself!*

Through sheer force of will, the verdant shoot tried to right herself, but her life force was depleted by the enormous energy consumed in withholding her rage and deep disappointment. Without this essential energy, the tiny plant would never flourish. She collapsed into her own exhaustion, flattened on the half-frozen earth, dead to the world and dead to herself.

As the days slipped by, the Little Green Flowering Essence lay placid on the now soft, warm earth. The old gardener finally noticed the misshapen flower. "Oh," he cried, kneeling close to her flattened figure, "what have I done to my poor beauty? I'm just a blind old clod, I am."

Spurred by his regret, the elderly man tried every trick he could dredge up from his storehouse of nursery wisdom to help the tiny green shoot stand upright in the sun. He packed extra dirt around her roots and watered her very carefully. He even positioned small stakes on either side of her stem for support. In spite of his best efforts, nothing worked.

As the tiny flower watched the old man try to make amends for his clumsiness and lack of vision, she scoffed at him in her mind. *If he thinks he can make up for what he did he's wrong! There's nothing he can do to make me feel better or help me stand tall. It's too late!*

Little Green Flowering Essence once again drooped over and lay motionless on the earth, the life force slipping ever so quickly, now, out of her being. The tiny green shoot began to wither and turn brown around the edges.

Just as the last ounce of life trickled from her cells, the little flower noticed a hint of warmth caress her slightly exposed roots. Her gaze was drawn upward, toward the source of that touch, the noonday sun. The sun smiled at the tiny sprout, showering the flower with loving radiance. "My child," the sun cooed, "you are an indispensable part of this garden. You must not relinquish hope."

The tiny shoot had forgotten the others. She briefly surveyed the landscape, and for the first time really noticed the dazzling beauty of wisteria overhanging the wood rail fence at the northern border, and the pink bleeding hearts partially protected by the towering lilacs on the eastern edge of the perennial bed. Suddenly, a deep longing to be part of this magnificence flowed from her roots. The Little Green Flowering Essence felt alive for the first time since that fateful day when she poked her head out the top of the deep vast earth, the womb of all creation.

The chlorophyll in the tiny flower's cells awakened and protoplasm flowed freely once again. Frozen feelings held tightly in check were instantaneously released as the little green shoot expired oxygen through her cells. Her wilted, brown edges turned green again. Then, in the wink of an eye, the Little Green Flowering Essence thrust her broken stem straight up from her roots and grew six inches taller.

The Flowering Essence grew rapidly, soon towering over the other plants in the garden. An enormous blossom emerged from the bud at the peak of her stalk, expanding into the shape of a bearded iris, deep crimson in color with gold splashes washing out over her petals. Her sword-shaped leaves came to attention and saluted the sun.

The Little Green Flowering Essence was now a lush and vibrant flower, as beautiful as any bloom that had ever graced the old English garden. All the other plants and flowers turned to the verdant being and applauded. "Welcome!" they cried. "Welcome to life!"

The Flowering Essence applauded in return and laughed a hearty laugh. A joyous celebration commemorating the glorious day was spontaneously launched by the Hollyhocks, joined quickly by all the other plants and flowers and followed shortly thereafter by the monarch butterflies, bumble bees, bugs, and even the ruby-throated hummingbird and his family.

Then, a stark silence crept over the garden. All creatures, great and small, held their breath as the shed door creaked open. The nurseryman gathered his tools and ambled over to the near corner of the perennial bed, where, by habit, he began his daily weeding. As he approached the Flowering Essence, an undisputed curl of horror spiraled up her stem. *Will he see me this time,* she wondered, *or will he crush me again?*

The Flowering Essence had forgotten that she had grown into a substantial and exquisite presence. It would have, indeed, been next to impossible to ignore her.

The elderly man stood, with mouth agape, before the Flowering Essence. At first, he didn't recognize her. "How on earth, my beauty, did you find your way into my garden?" Then he realized that she was the same flower he had trampled in his haste to rearrange the mulch, that first day of spring.

The seasoned nurseryman stood absolutely still, then reached out tenderly to the blossom and took in her fragrance with deep, full breaths. A single tear rolled down his cheek.

He pulled her gently toward his heart and whispered, "I'm so glad you're alive. Your beauty and grace fill my old eyes with joy. Please forgive me for my clumsiness and poor vision that nearly crushed the life out of you."

With these words, the Flowering Essence grew two feet taller. "Oh," the nurseryman laughed, "so you forgive me, now, do you?" He began to sing a silly old tune, then turned a jig for all the plants and creatures of the garden to see. They roared with delight, then joined in the dance.

As the Flowering Essence watched the festivities, she knew in her heart she had forgiven the old man. Delight tickled the flower's senses. As she watched the ancient figure dance with life, she heard a clear voice of freedom rise up from her roots. *Not only do I forgive you, but in an odd sort of way I'm grateful for your clumsiness. Because of my struggle, I am stronger, now-- a more glorious presence than I could've ever imagined.*

With those thoughts, the Flowering Essence, joined in the celebration. She opened her deep crimson blossom to the warmth of the sun, the joy of her life, and the fulfillment of relationship with all the other plants and creatures and, most especially, to the old man of the garden.

THE CAVE DWELLER

ong ago, during an age of forgetting, before Man divided time into fragments in a vain effort to control it, lived a tiny winged creature in a cave so dark you couldn't see your hand in front of your face. The air inside was oppressive. Each inhale felt as if the weight of the world's suffering was pressing in on your lungs. This smallest of creatures had always lived in the cave. She couldn't remember why or how she happened to be there. In fact, she didn't know much of anything. But she did know, somewhere deep in her heart of hearts, that she just didn't belong in that terrible place. It wasn't her real home.

The tiny being had only one clear memory. Sadly for her, it was a frightening experience she wanted to forget. But the harder she tried to push it away, the more it crowded in on her, until finally, the memory took up all the space in her mind.

Sometime in the distant past, an enormous monster had reached out from the shadows with his powerful, leathery hands, grabbed the startled creature, crushed her wings and roared, "Now you are mine forever! You'll never leave my lair!"

Now, having lived so long in forgetting, the creature couldn't even remember the monster's face. And even though she couldn't see her jailer, the wounded creature sensed his presence, rustling in the dark, waiting... She waited, too, waited vigilantly for his next attack.

But another attack never came. So the tiny being endured the waiting, the not knowing what might happen next, wrapped in a cloak of fear, frozen in time.

The creature lay trembling on the cold, hard floor of the cave, curled into a ball, barely breathing, hoping the monster would believe she was dead. And, in a manner of speaking, she was dead... for the life force of the tiny winged creature drained slowly, steadily from the cells of her body. She became the fear she felt.

This smallest of cave dwellers just barely survived in, what seemed to her, an eternity of terror. Then, one day, for no reason the tiny creature could explain, her attention was drawn away from her thought-cluttered mind toward a pulsing sensation inside her crumpled body. *This is strange. It's so cold in this cave, but I'm feeling very warm.*

Suddenly, the tiny creature heard a voice that seemed to come from the center of the pulsation. "Move," it said, "move toward the light." The cave dweller was curious about this message. She wasn't sure what it meant, but hearing these words triggered a feeling in her tiniest of hearts that could only be described as a longing, a calling. Now there was meaning, a sense of purpose.

As this inner desire grew, the cave dweller began to crawl around the cold, hard floor of the cavern, searching for something. But she didn't quite know what she was looking for. She thought, *I don't even know what "the light" is. I don't remember.*

This exploration seemed dangerous to the tiny creature, but she kept moving anyway. She assumed the monster had set snares and traps throughout the cave, so that no living being could escape.

Without warning, the cave dweller tumbled, head over heals, into a deep hole, a place of still greater darkness. The despairing creature thought, *that's what I get for trying! What's the point of trying to escape? He'll just trap me again and again. I'll just be worse off than I was before!*

The winged creature was on the verge of giving up when she heard the inner voice again, "Don't let him stop you. Follow your longing." The cave dweller was shocked to hear her own voice echo off the jagged walls in response, "Yeah! That's right. I'm not going to let any old monster or a few holes stop me."

From within a hidden recess of the creature's body arose a faint spark of anger. Then the anger turned to rage and the rage became a fiery passion. She called out a challenge to her invisible captor, "I've lived in fear too long. Enough! Just try and build a trap clever enough to keep me in this darkness one minute more."

Suddenly, as if awakened from a deep sleep, the winged being remembered the way out of the cave. The tiny creature crawled up the rough side of the hole. As she moved forward, slowly, with great care, the creature's longing acted like a beacon. Using her internal awareness and motivated by her sense of mission, the cave dweller navigated the maze of booby traps and obstacles that suddenly appeared before her, until she noticed a pinpoint of light in the distance. It was the entrance to the cave.

The next thing she knew, the cave dweller stood breathless and bedazzled in the radiance of the midday sun, the cloud of forgetting lifted from her mind. "Now I remember," she cried. "I remember how I ended up in that dreadful place."

Hundreds of thousands of years ago, the tiny being had noticed the entrance to the cave on one of her daily excursions around the fragrant, rainbow-colored wildflower garden in her backyard. She became curious about the darkness inside. Filled with a deep desire to explore its interior, the creature followed her longing into the heart of that alien world. Once inside, she was enveloped by a thick cloud of forgetting and quickly lost her way.

With this insight, the cave dweller unfurled her wings and flew straight toward the smiling sun who was nestled in the loving embrace of the brilliant blue sky. When she looked at herself in the light, the creature's heart skipped a beat. "Look at me!" she cried, recognizing her real self after so many years, "I'm a hummingbird!" Indeed, the once lost and crumpled creature was an iridescent harbinger of joy, dressed in green and red, reflecting the sun's glory back to the world with each turn of her agile body. A hummingbird... unmatched in the universe, for speed and power, by any other creature her size.

Released from the fear that had tortured her for years, the iridescent dart zipped here and there on the tiniest breath of air, burning with a new sense of freedom. Just then, some of the other creatures in the meadow, including Mr. and Mrs. Cardinal, Charlie the bumblebee and Sigmund the squirrel, craned their necks and turned their eyes upward, trying to catch a glimpse of her splendor. The rest of the meadow community looked up and applauded, dazzled by the light reflected off her tiny feathers.

In that moment, a deep passion rose up from the hummingbird's tiny belly. *I followed my longing into the cave,* she thought, *and I followed it out again. Now I must go back inside and tell the others who are still trapped there. I must tell them the truth!* The hummingbird darted back into the darkness. This time, however, when the cloud of forgetting enveloped her, she passed through it easily, following her desire into the heart of the cave.

She hurriedly gathered the other cave dwellers around her. They were astonished to witness a figure of such radiance and grace. In a tiny, yet enthusiastic voice, the hummingbird proclaimed, "You are not trapped in the darkness. You know the way out. Each of you chose to enter the cave a long time ago. You've just forgotten your passion and lost your way."

The others stared at the hummingbird, regarding her with mistrust. "You must be crazy!" they shouted. "Why would anyone *choose* to live in the dark?" The tiny winged being was not daunted by this skepticism.

"You are not helpless victims of fate," she stated calmly. "You chose this existence, but then you forgot. Now I'm here to tell you there's another way. You don't have to wait around anymore to see if the monster is going to crush you or spare you. You all know the way out! Just follow your own longing."

Suddenly, an enormous figure jumped out from the shadow. It was the monster. The ferocious beast confronted the hummingbird. "Lies!" he shouted. "You're telling them lies." He tried to smash her to the floor, but she was too quick.

Then self-doubt crept back into the tiny creature's consciousness. *Maybe he's right,* she thought, *I'm no match for a monster that big.*

The hummingbird hesitated, but before the cloud of forgetting could take over her mind, her inner voice chimed in, "You know the truth. Follow your longing."

The hummingbird laughed, then turned toward the beast and said, "I know who you really are! I made you up. You're just a thought in my brain; then I started to believe you were real. Go away! You can't hurt us now."

Having lost his power to dominate and control, the monster of the cave simply disappeared. "Poof!"

The assembly of cave dwellers applauded the hummingbird's bravery and ingenuity. She received their gratitude, then said, "Open your hearts and follow your own longing to safety. I'll help anyone who gets lost."

When the entourage reached the mouth of the cave, they were bathed in the brilliance of the fiery sun. The former cave dwellers thanked the tiny hummingbird for speaking the truth and persisting, even when they didn't believe her.

With that, the former cave dwellers joined hands in a circle and gave thanks to the light of truth. The hummingbird of joy darted overhead briefly, waved goodbye, then flew off to find another cave.

ZARTU AND THE HAEMON

I n the great ocean beyond the western shores of Armuton, lived a large pod of black and white whales known as Orcinus Orca. The Orca were passionate creatures with a reputation for being powerful and fierce predators. However, they were also gregarious, with a deeply ingrained sense of community. Although fearsome, they followed the law of the sea, taking only what they needed from their environment to ensure the survival of the pod.

These magnificent whales roamed freely over the great oceans with their dark, triangular-shaped dorsal fins looming six feet above the surface of the water, slicing through steep waves as a knife cuts butter. Their only natural enemy was the two-legged being known as Haemon.

Although the Haemon feared the mighty Orca, they envied their beauty, intelligence, and power. Small bands of two-leggeds hunted the Orca with nets and ropes, capturing and caging them in small pens. Then they'd charge other Haemon ten pieces of gold to watch the whales perform entertaining tricks like jumping through hoops for their supper. Thousands of two-leggeds flocked to these watery circuses to view the mighty beasts who'd been conquered by the even mightier Haemon.

The two-leggeds frequently explored the vast seas in their powerful, ocean-going vessels. searching for young or vulnerable Orca to snatch. Ironically, the Haemon lived on Terranfirm, walked upright on the ground and were terrified of the watery world the whales called home. However, safely situated on their ships, the two-leggeds never had to touch the liquidy depths.

When a Haemon craft approached a pod, the two-legged beings would single-out a whale, then quickly drop a large net. If the Orca, who was immediately entangled, struggled too hard, the lead harpooner would simply kill him, hurling his long, barbed spear into the helpless whale's heart.

The two-leggeds would then take the teeth, which could be sold as curiosities, and leave the remains floating in a pool of red to be picked apart by the scavengers of the sea.

One clear, crisp autumn afternoon, Zartu, a young whale and a group of his male friends wandered off from the rest of the pod in search of adventure. The whales busied themselves diving and breaching, chasing each other through kelp beds and playing hide and seek in the coral reef. Their favorite game was a competition to see who could propel his sleek, powerful body vertically out of the water, then make the biggest splash on touch down.

The juveniles were unaware of a Haemon vessel speeding full sail towards them. They were easy targets for the two-leggeds who had spotted their splashes from quite a distance.

Suddenly, Zartu sensed the familiar, yet threatening vibration of a Haemon harpoon boat tearing through the water. He sounded the Orca warning cry, a short energetic burst of clicks. Before the whales could disperse and dive, the speedy craft was on top of them.

From the bow of the boat, Zartu heard the two-leggeds screaming, "Look, there's one of those killer whales... Let's kill him before he kills us!"

"No," another shouted, "He's worth a lot more to us alive, if we can control him. We'll sell him to the sea circus."

Zartu was startled by the Haemon's brutality. He thought, *why do they hate me so much? I've never done anything to them!*

His heart broke open, as if the harpooner had already found his mark. The young Orca cried, "You're breaking the law of the sea! I'm not just some thing, I'm a real, living being!"

The Haemon ignored the youth's plea. In the next instant, Zartu felt the heavy weight of a net over his head. The pain in his heart suddenly became a ragged and fierce rage, coursing through his veins like a mighty river overflowing its banks.

He yanked the net sharply with his teeth and dragged a two-legged overboard. The young Orca freed himself from the trap and lunged at the terrified Haemon who gasped for breath, as he thrashed about, screaming and gulping salt water.

Just as Zartu reached the two-legged, Karmok, one of Zartu's closest friends, jabbed the rage-filled whale sharply in the ribs, diverting him from his helpless prey. Zartu turned to his friend and lashed out, "Why'd you do that. I was just about to tear him to shreds!"

Karmok looked sternly at his podmate and snapped, "Unlike the Haemon, we don't kill for profit or revenge! Let's get out of here. We've got to get back to the pod and warn the others."

As Zartu crashed through the waves, he pondered Karmok's remark... *but why do they call us "killers"?*

When the young whale finally returned to the safety of the pod, he decided to seek the counsel of the wise, old whale, Grampoys. As the esteemed elder of the community, his task was to guide and teach the younger Orca. Zartu thought, *if anyone can answer my question, Grampoys can.*

When he spied the old whale, the juvenile called out, "Grampoys, sir, do you have a moment? I have a question for you."

The elder replied, "Of course, my son, what can I do for you?"

Zartu recounted, in great detail and with much embellishment, the story of his painful encounter with the Haemon. "Grampoys, I really wanted to kill that Haemon, but Karmok stopped me. I felt like I would die from the pain in my heart, so all I could think about was killing him first to get rid of that awful feeling."

Then the young whale asked, "Why, sir, do the Haemon call us 'killers'? And why do they hate us so much?"

Grampoys sighed. The frown on the old whale's face suggested the churning in the pit of his stomach. He took a deep breath and replied, "My son, this is truly a sad day. You have been forced to learn a bitter lesson at such a vulnerable age. However, the truth is the truth, and the truth will always set you free. I would be happy to answer your questions. But first, let me take you to a sacred place at the bottom of the ocean. There, in the safety of that space, you may find the answers you seek."

The elder broadcast a series of clicks and tones, instructing the young whale to inhale several long, deep breaths. Grampoys transmitted a few more high-pitched tones, then they plummeted straight down into the ocean depths.

As they dove deeper and deeper into the unknown, a curious thing happened. The bluish-green water turned crimson red. Terrified, Zartu turned to Grampoys for help. "I'm scared, Grampoys!"

The old whale nuzzled the youth lightly with his nose and said, "Just take a deep breath."

"But Grampoys," the young whale protested, "I can't breathe down here. I'd have to surface to get air."

Grampoys remained calm. "Trust me. Go ahead and breathe."

Much to Zartu's amazement, as he opened the blow hole on the top of his head, fresh air, not water, poured into his lungs.

The youth's eyes popped wide open. "Grampoys," he cried, "this is great. I can breathe underwater. At least I think we're underwater. I've never been on a dive like this before."

As the youth breathed in the red all around him, he noticed strange, yet delightful sensations pulsating through his body. Suddenly, the pulsing turned to anger, then the anger turned to rage and the rage became a fiery passion, which just as quickly returned to a delightful pulsing. In that instant, the young whale felt more alive than he'd ever felt before.

As the elder and the youth dove deeper and deeper, they swam through every color of the rainbow. As Zartu inhaled each color, different sensations emerged in his awareness. As long as the young Orca kept breathing, he flowed through his feelings with the ease and grace of the sun merging with the sea at the edge of night, beyond the western horizon.

"Grampoys," he cried, "It's not so bad to feel hurt or angry down here."

Grampoys smiled. When they reached the silky bottom, the old whale led the youth to the mouth of a cave. Zartu noticed a shaft of light in the distance. The pair swam through the entryway and followed the light down a long tunnel, where they finally surfaced in an underwater cavern. Sprouting from the walls and floor and ceiling were millions upon millions of multi-faceted crystals, sparkling in dazzling shades of pink, purple, orange and green.

Grampoys and Zartu rested wearily on the surface of the water in the heart of the enchanted cave. Suddenly, a brilliant white light radiated from one of the crystals, then echoed back and forth among the other stones. Graceful harmonics reverberated throughout the cave. This awe-inspiring symphony of light and sound enveloped the two travelers in an aura of tranquility.

When the music stopped, Grampoys turned to his youthful companion and said, "Now that we're in the sanctuary, I'll answer all of your questions."

The astonished juvenile could hardly speak. "Ss... sir, wh... where are we? What is this place?"

Grampoys smiled. "My son, this is your own inner sanctum. It's quite splendid, isn't it."

Zartu's huge, toothed jaw dropped open. He blushed so badly the white patches on his body turned a deep, dark pink. "Yes, it's beautiful... I had no idea."

Grampoys replied, "Well, of course you had no idea. It's not that easy to catch a glimpse of your real self, in all its grandeur. It takes courage and commitment to dive this deep inside. But here you are, and this is the real you."

"Really, Grampoys?"

"Yes, really."

Once the shock of witnessing his inner beauty faded, Zartu's thoughts turned to his encounter with the Haemon. "Grampoys, please tell me why the two-leggeds hate the Orca? Why do they call us 'killers' and try to trap us?"

Grampoys replied, "You see, my son, the Haemon reject the law of the sea which says, 'All things come from one thing. So take only what you need and honor what you take.' They're afraid to become part of the great cycle of life because it would mean admitting that they are not as powerful or invulnerable as they'd like to believe. They both fear and covet our power, which is the power of love and the acceptance of our place in the family of things. So they make us objects of hate, making it easier to justify their cruelty."

"But that's not fair," exclaimed Zartu. "That makes me want to kill them first!"

"Ah, but you see, my dear son," Grampoys interjected, "then you become just like them, caught in the all or nothing thinking of 'it's either me or you,' when the truth is 'all things come from one thing.' If you kill them for revenge, you'll experience a much deeper pain than the wound from their taunts or harpoons. You'll feel the pain of separation from everything that is sacred. Life feeds on life, but if you kill in violation of the law of the sea, you'll truly be a 'killer,' separated from your own inner beauty."

The elder continued, "As difficult as it may be, we must learn to open our hearts to the two-leggeds. They live in a world of denial and distorted truth."

Zartu tried to take in the wisdom of his mentor. Then he asked, "But, sir, what do I do with my impulse to strike back?"

"Let me show you, Zartu."

"Okay."

"Close your eyes, my son, and take a deep breath. Now remember the incident with the Haemon."

Zartu squirmed with discomfort. "I feel that awful pain, Grampoys. I hate it! I want to kill him. I want to tear him apart!"

Suddenly the walls of the cavern reverberated with an ear splitting noise radiating from the crystals. Zartu opened his eyes, the cave was as black as a moonless night.

"Grampoys," the frightened youth cried, "what happened?"

"This is what happens when you violate the law of the sea. You hear the dissonance of untruth and can no longer see your inner beauty."

"This is terrible, Grampoys. How can I get it back?"

The old whale touched the young Orca lightly with his fin and replied, "Remember the incident again, but this time feel the pain. Stay with the truth of your experience."

Zartu closed his eyes. His heart heaved open. "Grampoys, I'm dying... I'm dying."

The old whale nuzzled the youth gently to remind him, "I'm right here, son. Remember how easy it was to swim through your feelings as we dove."

Zartu took several deep breaths. Suddenly he saw the image of the helpless Haemon thrashing about in the water. A river of tears washed the rage from the young Orca's eyes. "When I look at the Haemon now, Grampoys, I just feel sad. I don't want to kill him anymore. It's so sad that he's afraid of me and wants to hurt me."

"That's right, my son. It's very sad."

Just then, the cavern filled to bursting with delightful harmonics. When Zartu opened his eyes this time, millions of multi-faceted crystals were beaming at him.

The wise old Orca looked lovingly into the young one's eyes and said, "Whenever you want to kill someone who's hurt you, dive down deep into the watery world of your own feelings and return to this sanctuary. Here you'll remember the truth of who you are, in relationship to the world. Then your actions will flow effortlessly from your own wisdom, in alignment with the law of the sea."

Zartu breathed a sigh of relief. His sleek black and white body expanded, his lungs filled with air and a wave of acceptance washed over his powerful frame. "Grampoys, your words make a sound in my heart just like the sound of these beautiful crystals. You're the wisest Orca in the whole world!"

They both laughed out loud, sending echoes of joyful sound bouncing wildly from one crystal to another, until the cave was filled with one huge laugh. The wise old whale gave his young student a pat on the back and said, "You've learned your lesson well. Now it's time to return to the pod."

Grampoys instructed the young Orca to close his eyes and breathe deeply once again. In the flap of a tail, Zartu emerged from the depths of his inner world into his everyday life. The wise, old whale was right beside him.

Grampoys winked at the youth, then sent the young Orca on his way with some final words. "Remember, the waters of emotion run deep... follow the light to your own inner beauty and there you will find the truth."

With that, Zartu propelled himself out of the water with his massive tail and turned a back flip. When he touched down, the weight of his body created a splash so tall it touched the edge of the sun. Then he raced toward the horizon, slicing through the waves of the great ocean beyond the western shores of Armuton.

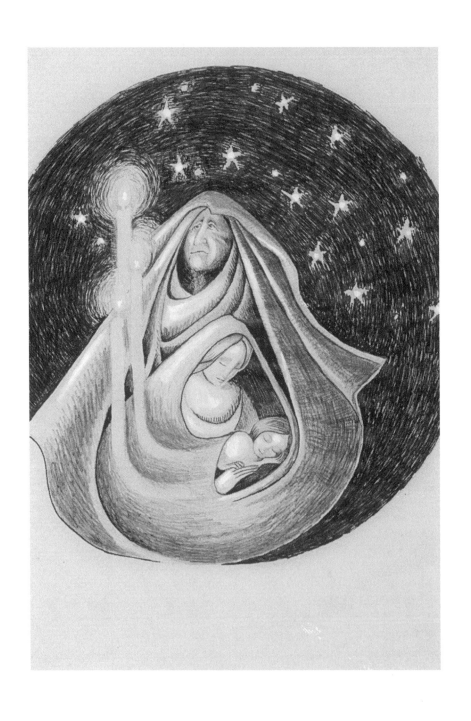

THE WAY HOME

C orine curled up underneath her soft, velvety pink blanket while her mother seated herself at the edge of the bed and opened the little girl's favorite book of fairy tales. Corine giggled in anticipation of hearing her mother's melodic voice. She relished these special times when she owned her mother's undivided attention. The engaging woman smiled at Corine and said, "Ah, here's a story you'll really like..."

"Once upon a time in a great kingdom on the far side of creation lived a little girl named Tess." Corine's mother laughed, then showed her daughter the picture of the little girl in the story. "Look," she said. "She looks just like you, with beautiful rosy cheeks, blue eyes and golden hair."

Corine's mother gazed at her precious daughter who was staring intently at the colorful illustration. She noticed a pleasant warmth envelop her heart.

She continued. "Tess was a very sad little girl. For you see, the kingdom on the far side of creation was covered in a thick, dark fog. Tess had never seen the sun, although she'd heard from some of the brave knights at court that it was possible to find the light if you journeyed far into the wilderness and overcame the demons who inhabited the fringes of the forest.

"Many knights traveled from the safety of the castle walls on this quest for the sun. Some never returned. Others returned broken, having failed to reach their goal. Then the other knights would sigh, bow their heads and whisper, 'Poor man, his heart was not pure enough.' Then they would retire to their chambers, hanging their heads in fear, wondering if their hearts were pure enough.

"One day Tess decided to go on a quest for the light. She knew the journey would be dangerous, but her deepest longing was to be bathed in the warm glow of the sun. She thought, *I know it's out there, somewhere... if I can just be very good and very pure, maybe I can find it!*

"Tess packed a small sack of food, snuck past the sentry posted at the front tower and raced out of the castle as fast as her young legs would carry her. She sprinted down the footpath that she thought led to the main road, but quickly lost her way in the dense fog. The little girl was soon gasping for breath. She collapsed on an old tree stump.

"She sobbed loudly, 'Oh, I'm lost, I'm lost... I'll never find the light. And now I'll never find my way home. Someone, please help me, I'm lost!' Just as she spoke these words a mysterious, lady, with long flowing golden hair and a magnificent magenta cape, appeared before the hapless girl. Her beauty dazzled the child.

"Tess gasped. As she stared at the ageless lady's soft blue eyes, the little girl noticed a creamy white stone, in the shape of a crescent moon, dangling from a shiny gold chain around her neck.

"The mysterious lady smiled gently at Tess and said, 'I heard you call out. I will gladly help you find your way home.'

"Tess clapped her hands. The enchanted lady sat down next to the girl, gently stroked her hair, then carefully placed her weary head in her lap and said,

'Take a deep breath, little one, and I will tell you a story that will help you find your way home.'"

Once upon a time there was a little Princess, just about your age, with golden hair and blue eyes, who wandered away from the castle looking for her canary yellow ribbon which she thought she had lost in the tournament field the day before during the joust.

It was her favorite ribbon and it made her feel so pretty when she wore it. She thought she'd just die if she couldn't find it.

So the Princess followed the path through the woods that led to the great tournament field... but, alas, she was soon lost in the forest. She felt scared and very foolish for leaving the safety of her home for a ribbon. All she wanted was to be home in front of a warm fire, sipping broth from her wooden bowl.

Just as the Princess thought this thought, a gnarled old dwarf came hobbling down the path, mumbling to himself. He was in a rush and nearly walked right past her, but she reached out, grabbed him by the arm and cried out, "Won't you please help me find my way home!" The ragged old dwarf jumped back and yelled, "Go away, leave me alone, I'll have no part of you or your problems!"

The bewildered Princess quickly held up a gold coin from her pouch and said, "If you show me the trail back to the castle, I'll give you a gold coin." The Dwarf's eyes lit up. He hastily grabbed the shiny coin, concealed it in his pocket and hobbled away as fast as his gnarled, old legs would carry him.

The Princess was deeply offended, then fell into despair, wondering aloud, "How am I ever going to find my way home if no one shows me the right path?"

As the day wore on, all manner of creatures and curious beings passed by the Princess on their way through the forest.

Each time a stranger approached, the Princess pleaded, with clasped hands, then offered a coin in return for their help.

Some of the passers-by simply stole her money and ran. Other travelers spent hours and hours revealing to her what they professed to be the great wisdom of the ages. Then they'd grab the coin and leave the little girl with an unsolvable riddle. Still others snatched the gold and led her down the wrong path. Finally the tired, frightened, and frustrated little girl was even more lost than before.

As the day waned and dusk settled over the land, the Princess collapsed. She was hungry, lonely, scared and lost. She curled up into a tight little ball on top of an old tree stump and cried herself to sleep.

When the Princess awoke, she looked up to the heavens and saw the moon, a creamy white orb in its fullness, shining her brilliant light over the world. Suddenly the Princess heard a sweet melodic voice emanating from the white glow, "Look inside your own heart. The answers you seek are there."

The Princess took a deep breath. She saw a bright light pour from her heart which illuminated her way back to the path where she first entered the forest. Then, much to her delight, the Princess saw the tower off in the distance. She used her heartlight, as a beacon, until she stood before the castle gate. She pounded on the giant wooden door and was eagerly welcomed home.

"Tess looked up at the mysterious lady and said, 'That was a wonderful story. I feel so much better. Now will you help me find my way home?'

"The enchanted woman smiled, looked lovingly into the girl's eyes and said, 'Of course. All you need to do is follow your own heartlight, just like the Princess in the story. Breathe deeply and surrender to the flow of life within you. Your heart will guide you home.'

"Tess followed the mysterious lady's instructions and suddenly saw, in her mind's eye, the correct path to the palace.

"Tess hugged the mysterious lady. 'Thank you! Thank you!' she cried, then bolted down the footpath, her journey through the dense fog illuminated by her own heartlight.

"As Tess approached the castle she stopped dead in her tracks. The palace and surrounding area were bathed in golden sunlight. The little girl's heart expanded further. She felt more alive than she'd ever felt before, as her own inner radiance poured out from her heart to meet the light of the sun.

"She laughed, 'Silly me, the light's been here the whole time, I've just been looking for it in the wrong place. The light's in me and now I'm home.'"

Corine's mother smiled and said, "... and that's the end of the story."

She lowered the book of fairy tales and glanced over at Corine. The tired little girl had fallen fast asleep. The loving mother leaned over, kissed her beloved daughter lightly on the forehead, tenderly stroked her hair, turned off the lamp by the bed and walked quietly out of the room.

In the next instant, Corine awoke abruptly to find herself sitting in a rocking chair in front of a blazing fire with a book in her lap, dazed and disoriented. She pondered aloud, "Why am I sitting in front of this fire when I should be in bed underneath my pink blanket... and where did my mother go?"

Then Corine looked down and saw the hands of a wrinkled old woman. "Ugh," she blurted, "I must have fallen asleep."

Not wanting to break the spell, the old woman sat very still, savoring the warmth of the fire, the comforting remembrance of snuggling underneath the covers, and the sound of her mother's voice.

The old woman sighed. A sharp pang of grief shot through her heart as another memory of her mother emerged in her awareness. *Fifteen years,* she thought. *It's been fifteen years tonight since she died.* Corine saw her mother lying in the hospital bed, emaciated, tubes in her arms, her last breath released from her lungs. Then she was gone. Just like that.

A moist softness collected around the old woman's eyes as she whispered to the night, "Oh, mother, I miss you. Sometimes I feel so lost without you."

Then, as if a fog lifted from her mind, the elderly woman remembered Tess and the castle and her quest for the light. She smiled and thought, *what a strange dream.*

Corine carefully pushed herself to standing with her cane, hobbled slowly over to the large picture window, opened the drapes, and stared out into a clear, cold mid-winter sky. She was dazzled by the stars twinkling bright against the dark, velvety texture of the night and the creamy white radiance of a waning moon. It was that soft, billowy light that reminded Corine of the mysterious lady.

As a single tear disappeared into a crack in the old woman's cheek, she thought, *how strange, all my life I've struggled, searching for someone to direct me, to answer my questions and solve my problems. All the time I've had the answers right here, inside of me.*

Corine drew up her nightgown slightly above her ankles, as she skillfully steadied herself with her cane, then cautiously climbed the stairway and negotiated the long corridor to her bedroom. She removed her slippers and draped her terrycloth robe over the foot of the bed. As she curled up underneath the covers, her two cats, Bridget and Ginger, snuggled up in the small of her back and purred, deep, comforting belly rumbles.

Corine dozed intermittently. When the old woman opened her eyes, she saw the mysterious lady from her dream in a sliver of moonlight that nudged its way through a crack in the drapes of the bedroom window. Then she heard that gentle, melodic voice, "Just remember... simply breathe deeply and surrender to the flow of life within you. Your own heart will always guide you home."

Corine sighed a deep, long sigh of relief, smiled gently at the lady and said, "Yes, I've finally found my way home."

EPILOGUE

I want to honor and acknowledge each of you for daring to delve inward to discover the divine and at the same time embrace the human self in all of its glory, as well as its pain and struggle.

If you surrender to the flow of life, the sacred spiral will lead you deeper and deeper into your true nature. As you approach each circle of the helix, you will be greeted by an ever increasing awareness of your own truth and inner beauty. It is my sincerest hope that these stories have illuminated a gateway to that truth.

These stories were born from the womb of my own experience and the wisdom of my own soul's journey. Part of that journey has been my participation in the Pathwork, an integrated process of spiritual development and transformation based on the Pathwork Guide Lectures. I wish to offer a special acknowledgement and my deepest thanks to the New York Region Pathwork, the Pathwork Foundation and the international Pathwork community. They have kept alive the spirit of Eva Pierrakos and the teachings of the Guide.

If you would like to know more about the Pathwork I recommend The Pathwork of Self-Transformation, by Eva Pierrakos, Bantam Books, New York, 1990.

With peace and blessings on your journey...

Patricia A. Burke
1995

ABOUT THE AUTHOR

Patricia A. Burke, MSW is a poet, story-teller, educator, and psychotherapist in private practice in Maine. She is the co-founder of the Beyond Mind Healing Center and a member of the New York Region Pathwork, a spiritual community founded on the teachings of the Guide. She is also a faculty member of the Rutgers University Summer School of Alcohol and Drug Studies and the Department of Social Work at the University of Southern Maine. Her other publications include, *The Great Frog Has No Preference* and *Hagen's New Name.*

ABOUT THE ILLUSTRATOR

Viki Kennedy lives in the woods of northern Maine with her husband John, who is a photographer, and their nine hybrid wolves.

Audenreed Press
1-888-315-0582
(Call Toll Free M-F 9-5 ET)

Order Form
𝔅reathe 𝔇eeply! 𝔋ealing 𝔖tories for the 𝔖oul

$12.00 each x quantity _____ = total _____
                  Maine residents 5.5% sales tax _____
Shipping & Handling
                  $2.00 (US book rate)
                  $4.00 (US priority mail)
                  $.50 each additional book _____
                                    Total _____

Send check to :   Audenreed Press
                        PMB 103
                        PO Box 1305
                        Brunswick, ME 04011
                        (207) 833-5016

Name _____

Address _____

_____

Phone _____

visit the 𝔅reathe 𝔇eeply! website at:
http://w3.ime.net/~bmhc/breathe.htm